Why Young People Don't Vote

Why Young People Don't Vote

Mitchell Agg

Winchester, UK
Washington, USA

First published by Zero Books, 2016
Zero Books is an imprint of John Hunt Publishing Ltd., Laurel House, Station Approach,
Alresford, Hants, SO24 9JH, UK
office1@jhpbooks.net
www.johnhuntpublishing.com
www.zero-books.net

For distributor details and how to order please visit the 'Ordering' section on our website.

Text copyright: Mitchell Agg 2015

ISBN: 978 1 78279 218 5
978 1 78279 246 8 (ebook)

A CIP catalogue record for this book is available from the British Library.

Design: Stuart Davies

Printed and bound by CPI Group (UK) Ltd, Croydon, CR0 4YY, UK

We operate a distinctive and ethical publishing philosophy in all
areas of our business, from our global network of authors to
production and worldwide distribution.

CONTENTS

Introduction

I was born in 1993 during the premiership of John Major. Therefore, I am part of the 18–24 year old demographic that records the lowest turnout at elections. In fact at the 2010 general election, it was eleven per cent lower than 25–34 year olds. But why the low turnout? Do young people just suddenly start following politics when they turn 25? Or is there more to it than that? In this book I will shed some light upon the issue of why young people tend not to vote. I am writing this at the height of the 2015 general election and political fever has gripped the country. Well, it has amongst UKIP supporters. The usual election fever hasn't bowled everyone over this time, as the meaningless choice between Labour and the Conservatives overshadows the entire event.

Although the press would have you believe that young people don't vote due to ignorance, I have broadened it to four main reasons. These are lies, corruption & cover-ups; broken system; disinterest, disillusionment & obliviousness; and lack of knowledge. Each one holds its own merits as to why young people don't vote, but at the end of the book I will conclude what I believe the main reason is.

But, before beginning the book, I want to share my political beliefs with you, the reader, so that you are aware of any political bias that may come across in my writing. At the age of 21, the 2015 general election was my first. As a self-proclaimed member of the left, I was part of the Green surge and was amongst the one million others that voted for the Green Party. Although I voted for them, I wouldn't necessarily affiliate myself with the party and I only did so because I felt they best represented my political beliefs. I was pleased with the number of votes that the Greens won, but the smell of the broken system lingered over the aftermath of the election for weeks. I am very pro-electoral reform and the introduction of a PR system, as I think many voters are.

I haven't always been left-wing. I'm not even sure how I'd define myself. It wasn't until about November 2014 when my political beliefs changed dramatically due to a certain comedian and his political activism. Yes, I am talking about Russell Brand. Although his message was originally telling people that there's no point in voting because there's nobody to vote for, it was his musings and activism on social injustice that changed the course of my political journey. Before Brand, I was the complete opposite of what I am today. At the 2014 local and European elections, I voted Conservative. My leaning was positively capitalist and I didn't pay much attention to the left.

Before writing this book, I conducted a mini survey of a hundred 18–24 year olds about why young people don't vote. The purpose of the survey was to give myself some context and a brief before jumping head-first into the subject matter. From the survey, I extracted quotes from numerous respondents and filtered them into the book for each chapter. Although the survey doesn't stand up against other professional and much larger surveys, I feel it does give each chapter something extra.

Chapter One

Lies, Corruption & Cover-Ups

I don't vote because I don't trust politicians.
- Tom, aged 21

During my research for this book, I conducted my own mini survey through social media to find out why people between the ages of 18 and 24 vote less than the rest of the population. The survey was answered by a range of people, some of whom did vote but the overwhelming majority of whom did not. These findings do not lay any foundation for statistical evidence as the pool is far too small. However, the results do correspond with polls done on a much larger scale by professional pollsters and media companies.

I asked the respondents if they trusted politicians. Here are the findings:

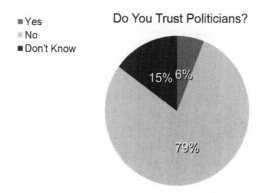

As you can see, out of the 100 young people I asked, a massive 79 per cent of respondents said that they don't trust politicians. I don't think that this is a surprising figure and I'm pretty certain that this percentage wouldn't decrease much if one widened the survey for all ages. The general public on the whole is disengaged and disenfranchised with politics because we are constantly being bombarded with news stories of politicians lying and cheating. Add to that, we see politicians not delivering what they promise in their manifestos or on the campaign trail. It's no wonder that we have such hate for politicians with all the bad press and ugly stories. And the problem is, the majority of young people only see the backend of the criticism. Unlike other demographics who read these stories in the paper or see it on the TV news where they are given the full raft of information to which they can ultimately decide their own personal viewpoint, the majority of young people will only see a headline in less than 140 characters on *Twitter* with a link to an article that they probably won't click. Is this the fault of the young people or the biased nature of the press? For instance, if a politician is accused of something with little evidence supporting the claim, most media companies will post a tweet slating the politician as if the claim had been proved true. Young people will see this retweeted onto their newsfeeds from numerous sources and take it as fact because they're not receiving the entire story. Although, most of the time, the general public's distrust is actually credible and just, and young people won't go out of their way to vote for politicians who are disloyal or corrupt.

Nick Clegg Lied to Us

There was no other unkept promise that young people felt so hurt by than Nick Clegg's vow to cut tuition fees during the 2010–2015 coalition. This is a direct quote from the Liberal Democrats' 2010 general election manifesto:

Scrap unfair university tuition fees for all students taking their first degree, including those studying part-time, saving them over £10,000 each. We have a financially responsible plan to phase fees

out over six years, so that the change is affordable even in these
difficult economic times, and without cutting university income.
We will immediately scrap fees for final year students.

We all know what happened next. On the back of gaining votes from young people who expected them to scrap university fees, the Liberal Democrats walked into a coalition with a party that firmly wanted to raise tuition fees. Not long into David Cameron's first year, the government announced that tuition fees would rise from £6,000 to the upper tier of £9,000 by 2012. Lo and behold, this was subsequently introduced and Nick Clegg and his party received a battering from students who had voted for him on the basis that fees would be cut. This had a dramatic effect on the Liberal Democrats in the 2014 European elections, overall membership of the party and the subsequent 2015 general election. In the 2007 European elections, the Lib Dems earned a 14 per cent share of the votes and won 11 seats in the European Parliament. After the formation of the coalition and the broken promise of tuition fees, the Lib Dems lost a total of 10 MEPs and took a mere 6 per cent share of the votes. They were left with a solitary MEP in Catherine Bearder who represents the South East of England.

This decline in votes isn't necessarily a direct result of the distrust for the Liberal Democrats, as many of the population have become Eurosceptic in their views and the Lib Dems are firmly pro-European. However, I think to overlook the distrust as a factor of their poor performance in these elections would be remarkably ignorant. There's also a direct correlation with the Lib Dems' performance in the local and European elections and their official membership numbers. At the time of the 2010 general election, according to their official figures the Liberal Democrats had 65,038 certified members. In the year of the intro-duction of greater tuition fees, their membership had decreased by almost 23,000 to 42,501 official members. The Liberal

Democrats suffered a disastrous blow in the 2015 general election, losing 49 seats and dropping to the fourth biggest party in terms of seats. In terms of popular vote, the Lib Dems won 2.4 million. That's a loss of 15 per cent since the 2010 election.

There's no denying that this was a direct reverberation of their broken promise. The general public felt aggrieved and took the stance that Nick Clegg and his party had lied through their teeth in their manifesto. Their decline in the 2015 general election shows the mood of the country: that we are fed-up with politicians lying. The break of the promise sealed this mood and enraged the public with many even voting for the Greens or UKIP as a form of protest.

Although the Liberal Democrats' membership is back on the rise, albeit in a position where they're no longer considered a major political party, I don't think young people will be as understanding as older voters because this broken pledge hit them directly. We live in a country where politicians are seen as liars and the first-time voters who supported Clegg found out firsthand that everything they had previously heard about politicians was true. The majority won't vote again. How can they trust another politician to deliver what they promise if they've seen the stereotype personally cheat them?

EU Referendum Promises

In 2009 David Cameron released a video stating the need for a referendum on Britain's involvement within the European Union. He referred back to Gordon Brown, who stated the need for a referendum in 2005 but failed to deliver. Cameron proposed that a referendum would come and said, prior to the European elections of 2009, "the best way to get that referendum is to vote conservative." One would assume that Cameron, being in power after this video, would have the chance to give the people of Britain a referendum on the EU. But this didn't happen, and instead, he used the promise of a referendum again in the run-up to the 2015 general election in order to sway voters away from UKIP. This is another example of deception by politicians, and this time it was two separate Prime Ministers, Brown and Cameron, both promising a referendum on Britain's membership of the EU and not delivering.

David Cameron made another promise whilst in opposition, again during the Brown administration. He convincingly affirmed that he would not raise VAT if he became Prime Minister in 2010. He promised this during an interview with Jeremy Paxman where he said "We have absolutely no plans to raise VAT." This was shortly followed by him saying the Conservatives' first budget would be about getting "spending under control rather than putting up tax." Then, during their very first budget, the Chancellor George Osbourne announced that VAT would be going up from 17.5 per cent to 20 per cent. Cameron clearly broke a promise that the electorate would've voted for him on. This promise not to raise VAT seems to get overlooked by Clegg's deviation on tuition fees, even though Cameron's promise affected more people and he was Prime Minister, whereas Clegg didn't win the election and his promise only affected students.

Cameron got away with breaking this promise until he was grilled again by Paxman in the run-up to the 2015 general election. Cameron had previously declared that they would not raise VAT again if the Conservatives won the election and Paxman stated "There's a whole credibility problem here isn't there?" Paxman then quoted Cameron's promise on VAT during the last election campaign and added "You said it to my face twice, at the time of the last election, and then the moment you got into government, you did raise VAT." Cameron responded by saying "There is a crucial difference on this occasion. We are the government. We've been able to look very carefully at the books and we know what is necessary in the next parliament and our plans do not involve tax increases on VAT." Cameron quite clearly showed no remorse about lying last time. His response was to suggest that somehow, if they had been in parliament during the Brown premiership, they would have been able to "look very carefully at the books." His lack of remorse for lying is sickening to most. This is where Clegg and Cameron differ hugely. We all quite clearly saw the remorse in Clegg when he released his apology video. Cameron didn't even say sorry for breaking his promise on VAT because, as far as he was concerned, we'd forgotten about it.

Young people are turned off by politics because they see events such as this: Politicians lying and cheating. And it's not just individual cases. The press are constantly bombarding us, and rightly so, with stories of corruption within the government. Can the press be blamed for turning young people against politicians? No, it's their job to inform us on these cases and it's the politicians themselves who need to stop lying and cheating and instead become figures of respectability. Young people will not get into politics if all they hear are stories of lying politicians. They're not going to vote for people who are as crooked as Gordon Gekko.

Boy Racer, Chris Huhne

In March 2013 the former Energy Secretary and former Liberal Democrat MP for Eastleigh, Chris Huhne, was sentenced to eight months in prison for perverting the course of justice along with his ex-wife Vicky Pryce. This is another example of why not just young people, but the general public, don't trust politicians. Huhne was caught speeding ten years prior to his jail sentence in March of 2003. Having previously already collected nine points on his license, he convinced the DVLA that his then wife, Vicky Pryce, was behind the wheel of the car when speeding on the M11 from Stansted Airport to London. After a messy breakup between

Huhne and Pryce, it came to surface that Huhne had swapped points with his wife to avoid being banned from driving. For over a year, the former Energy Secretary protested his innocence. Evidence came to light in the form of text messages between the Lib Dem MP and his son Peter Huhne. On 21st May 2003, Huhne's son sent the following message to his father:

We all know you were driving and you put pressure on mum. Accept it or face the consequences. You've told me that was the case. Or will this be another lie.

When this evidence was brought up, Huhne stated that his son was "taking his mother's side." Along with this piece of evidence, the court also ruled that nobody else could've been viably driving the car at the time. With concrete evidence against him, Huhne decided to eventually give up the ghost and change his plea to guilty. After he and his wife served less than two of the eight months inside, they were both release on probation. In a subsequent interview with *Channel 4 News*, Huhne said the following about the situation:

Sorry to my family, friends, colleagues and constituents. Very clearly, I should not have swapped points with my wife... It was a very stupid thing to do and I very much regret doing it.

Huhne also went on to call the act of swapping points a "trivial issue." Although Huhne will never work in politics again, it does raise the issue quite soundly of trust in politicians. Huhne didn't have to apologise. There was nothing he could say that would turn opinion back on his side. Moreover, there wasn't anything he could say that would make people trust him ever again. If by nature you lie about your whereabouts to cheat a government body in the DVLA, you shouldn't be a public servant in the form of an MP or a government minister. Not even his own son can trust him, as seen in the text message. This was a high-profile case and was covered intensely across the media for its entirety. There was no hiding from this story and all it did was prove to the already disengaged public that politicians are liars and cheats. Amazingly, this wasn't the first time Huhne was found out to be a crook. Although the feeling of public disengagement with politicians had been rife for many years leading up to now, it was the expenses scandal that really turned us against politics.

The Expenses Scandal

In May 2009, the *Daily Telegraph* served the public's interests and lifted the curtain on MPs' expenses. Prior to his scandal with the courts, Chris Huhne was one of the many MPs guilty of wrongly claiming expenses. Huhne used the system to purchase groceries, fluffy dusters and a trouser press of all things. When uncovered, Huhne stated that he would repay the cost of the trouser press in order to "avoid controversy" but didn't repay for his groceries or fluffy duster. The most outrageous and extraordinary claim above all other in this expenses scandal was by the Conservative MP Douglas Hogg, also known as the Viscount of Hailsham. He allegedly claimed £2,115 to have his moat at his country estate cleaned. He also claimed to have his piano tuned and hired a gardener all with government expenses. The former Sleaford and North Hykeham MP denied the allegations, saying "I have never claimed for the moat, or for the piano tuning – the allegation that I did is incorrect. I never claimed for these and I never received any money."

The fact that a member of parliament was accused of such crookery isn't surprising to most. Nor is the fact that we don't know whether we can believe his rejection of the allegation. If true, the fact that an MP claimed for such things truly shows the class divide in our society. The entire fiasco turned Westminster into a laughing stock and the funniest thing about the entire expenses scandal is how it was the richest MPs, with the poshest-sounding names, who filled the most expenses. We may not know whether Mr Hogg did claim to have his moat cleaned but our trust in politicians will continue to decrease because we see stories like this. If we don't know if they're telling the truth about this, how can we trust anything that they say in their manifestos?

Another Conservative who made a ridiculous claim was the former MP for Gosport, Sir Peter Viggers. According to the *Daily Telegraph*, Viggers was said to have claimed £30,000 on gardening over a period of three years. Part of this claim was to purchase a pond feature costing £1,645. It was later revealed that this 'pond feature' was in fact a 5ft floating duck island. Sir Peter Viggers, who was knighted in 2008, didn't go out of his way to deny the allegations but released this statement on his personal website: "Personally, I have of course always scrupulously observed the rules." His failure to deny the allegation directly poured more gasoline onto the fire of discontent for politics.

Hogg and Viggers weren't the only two politicians who made outrageous claims. The Conservative MP for North East Hampshire, James Arbuthnot, claimed £43 for three garlic peeling and cutting sets, the Conservative MP for Old Bexley and Sidcup, Derek Conway, claimed £97 for two toilet seats and the former Conservative MP for Wells, David Heathcoat-Amory, claimed £380 for horse manure. Although Arbuthnot, Conway, Heathcoat-Amory, Hogg and Viggers were all Conservative politicians, the expenses scandal rocked all three main parties as well as Sinn Féin and the House of Lords.

The majority of politicians who were hit by the expenses scandal had made claims for second homes and house repairs. This included Labour's Keith Vaz who claimed £75,000 for a second house in Westminster even though his other property was a mere 12 miles away in Stanmore, West London. The then Home Secretary, Jacqui Smith, claimed £116,000 in Additional Cost Allowance over the period of several years. She had listed her second home as her house in Redditch, Worcestershire and listed her main home as the one in London where she lived with her sister. The reason for the outcry was because as the Home Secretary, she was eligible for a house in Westminster and didn't need to claim expenses to live with her sister. It was also alleged that Smith only spent three nights a week in her main home. The case was subsequently thrown out but a month after these allegations, Smith was hit by a new expenses scandal. The *Sunday Express* revealed that Smith had claimed £10 for two pornographic films on a pay-per-view channel. It came to light that her husband, Richard Timney, purchased the adult films when Smith was away from their home in Redditch. Both Smith and Timney apologised for the error and Smith paid back the claim. Although Smith herself can't be blamed for her husband's error, the entire expenses scandal emphasised the corruption and greed that we've all heard about before but didn't necessarily have any evidence of. The timing of the scandal was in conjunction with the financial crisis, which made the public even angrier. People were losing their jobs and many couldn't afford to pay their rent, whilst they saw these stories of MPs wrongly claiming thousands of pounds. Public disillusionment with politics was at an all-time low.

Do You Have a Job? Yes, I Have Two.

"I have to earn my income but when I'm not doing something, I can do what I like." The infamous words of the Conservative MP for Kensington Sir Malcolm Rifkind. This statement, caught on secret camera by Channel Four's *Dispatches*, raised the issue of MPs having second jobs. After a ten-per-cent pay rise in July 2015, an MP earns a salary of £74,000 a year. (Correct at time of publication.) He or she then has the opportunity to work a second job and many work as lawyers, company directors, doctors, farmers, lecturers or appear in the media for a fee. Others also receive "gifts" or "donations" whereas some hold land or property. Any extra income must be declared against their wage for being an MP and there is no cap on how much extra they can earn. According to the Register of Financial Interests, twenty MPs declared more £100,000 on top of their £67,000 salary in 2014.

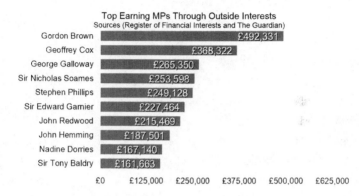

Top Earning MPs Through Outside Interests
Sources (Register of Financial Interests and The Guardian)

Gordon Brown	£492,331
Geoffrey Cox	£368,322
George Galloway	£265,350
Sir Nicholas Soames	£253,598
Stephen Phillips	£249,128
Sir Edward Garnier	£227,464
John Redwood	£215,469
John Hemming	£187,501
Nadine Dorries	£167,140
Sir Tony Baldry	£161,663

£0   £125,000   £250,000   £375,000   £500,000   £625,000

From these figures, it's no wonder that many young people and the rest of the general public think that politicians are only in it for themselves. Many argue that being an MP is a full-time job and those who take second jobs don't have the interest of their constituents at heart. There are some politicians who appear consistently on television and receive a fee for their appearance. The Labour MP for Hackney North and Stoke Newington, Diane Abbott, regularly appears on *This Week* with Andrew Neil. In 2014, *Guido Fawkes* reported that Abbott had earned £110,000 for appearances on the BBC since 2007. This revelation came two years after the BBC Trust admitted that Abbott had earned far too much and appeared far too frequently on *This Week*.

Some argue that there's a clear difference between media appearances and directorships or being a lawyer. However, whose job should it be to decide which jobs should stay and which jobs shouldn't be allowed? The debate about second jobs was brought up in parliament and the Prime Minister David

Cameron was questioned by his former opposite number, Ed Miliband, on the subject of second jobs. Miliband argued that MPs shouldn't be allowed second jobs and that if they do have them, the amount they can earn should not exceed 15 per cent of their salary as an MP. Cameron's responded by saying "I think parliament is stronger when we have people with different experiences come to our house." Many would argue that Cameron didn't want to upset the high-earning Conservative backbenchers who would've been in uproar if he'd agreed with the leader of the Labour party. According to a *YouGov* poll, 60 per cent of people believe being an MP should be a full-time job. It's no surprise when the average wage in the UK is £26,500 a year and for 18–24 year olds it's less than that by over £10,000. Not only that, but the average person can't have a second job to boost their income, let alone a second job that pays more than their basic salary. People won't vote for politicians who scandalously get away with milking the system and earning as much as they can fit in their pockets. Again, there are MPs who don't earn thousands extra from second jobs but the distinction isn't clear.

The Chilcot Inquiry

On 15th June 2009, the then Prime Minister Gordon Brown announced that an inquiry would be commissioned regarding Britain's role in the Iraq War. The inquiry was to be chaired by Lord John Chilcot, giving it the name 'the Chilcot Inquiry'. He and the other committee members were tasked to investigate Britain's involvement in Iraq between 2001 and 2009. Many believe that the Iraq War was illegal. Moreover, many believe that the then Prime Minister Tony Blair misled parliament with evidence that was less than watertight. The Blair government, along with the Bush administration, told the world that there was reason to believe that the President of Iraq, Saddam Hussein, had 'weapons of mass destruction' or 'WMD' for short. The suggestion of WMD frightened the world at the time but sceptics believed that Blair's evidence suggesting the existence of WMD was caustic. As did the 3,000,000 people who marched in London to urge the government not to go to war over minuscule and dodgy evidence.

When Alastair Campbell, who was the Director of Communications and Strategy under Blair during the Iraq War, appeared on Andrew Marr in 2010, he said, after overcoming tears, "I don't think people are interested in the truth anymore, Andrew. I think you're all interested in settling your scores and setting your own agenda." He then went on to say how he was there with Tony Blair and saw how tough the decision for war was. What Campbell said does hold some truth. For the Conservative party anyway. When the decision to go to war was made, the Tories backed Blair unashamedly. However, since they regained power under Cameron, they seemed to have forgotten which side of the fence they were on and, as Campbell suggested, it's like they merely wanted to settle scores and punch Labour whilst they were down.

However, the truth is wanted by the general public and Campbell's sweeping remarks are certainly not true for ordinary people. The inquiry took two years to document and we were expecting to see the release of the million-word report in 2014. However, difficult negotiations with the United States halted the release of the document as they disputed which private matters should be made public. The same problems hindered the report in the first place as in 2012, the government vetoed the release of documents to the inquiry detailing minutes of cabinet meetings regarding the Iraq invasion of 2003. They and the US government were agitated about what should be made public due to fears of national security. The report was the put back further by Lord Wallace of Saltaire as he stated it would be "inappropriate" to release the document months before the 2015 general election. The failure to release the document has made the public irate with the government. Many were left wondering what they were trying to hide from the general public. And it hasn't been cheap. According to sources, the Chilcot Inquiry has cost the British tax payers £9million. The Iraq Inquiry has made the British people even more sceptical about the British government and their eagerness to hide information from the public.

Andrew Mitchell and the Tale of the Plebs

Politicians just don't seem to stay away from controversy and young people are deterred when they see the stories in the papers or on their social feeds. A prime example of this was 'Plebgate', 'Plodgate' and, as *The Week* magazine referred to it, 'Gategate'. The suspicious incident, involving the then Chief Whip Andrew Mitchell and the police, was in the headlines for months. It occurred when the conservative MP for Sutton Coldfield was leaving 10 Downing Street on his bicycle. Allegedly, the police officers wouldn't open the gate for Mitchell and he became quite irate. According to reports, he then called the police officers "plebs." Mitchell reputedly denied calling the officers any such thing but did suggest that he "did not treat the police with the respect they deserve." This isn't what you'd expect to hear from an MP, nor were his alleged actions towards police officers. It's this type of conduct that puts people off voting for politicians. Andrew Mitchell was under pressure to resign for over a month after the incident and finally tendered his resignation as Chief Whip where he wrote:

> *I have made clear to you – and I give you my categorical assurance again – that I did not, never have, and never would call a police officer a "pleb" or a "moron" or used any of the other pejorative descriptions attributed to me. The offending comment and the reason for my apology to the police was my parting remark "I thought you guys were supposed to fucking help us". It was obviously wrong of*

me to use such bad language and I am very sorry about it and grateful to the police officer for accepting my apology.

Cameron accepted Mitchell's resignation and stated "incident in Downing Street was not acceptable and you were right to apologise for it." However, it eventually came to light that the officers may not have been telling the truth about the affair and another officer, PC Keith Wallis, was found to have falsely claimed to have witnessed the event. Wallis was sentenced to 12 months in prison and the other officers were asked by David Cameron, amongst others, to apologise to Mitchell. They subsequently apologised for "misleading the public." Mitchell appeared on *Channel Four News* where he declared that he was "stitched up by armed police officers." He also pointed out that the essence of the stickup meant that he, a cabinet minister, couldn't accuse the British Police Force of lying. Although 'plebgate' may have been taken out of proportion and the accusations may not have been truthful, it's the mere fact of being in that position as a politician that is unacceptable. It adds to further disengagement from the public as they see politicians acting as if they're better than the general public and the police in this instance. Mitchell probably did lose his ministerial job unfairly but the public don't want people in power who act in his manner. Moreover, the investigation cost the British tax payers a huge £237,000 – money that could've been spent elsewhere and put to better use.

Once Upon a Time There Lived a Bigot Named Gillian Duffy

During Brown's premiership, scandals and mistakes weren't uncommon. He himself as Prime Minister wasn't far from controversy. In the run-up to the 2010 general election, Gordon Brown visited Rochdale on 28th April. Whilst there, he encountered a

65-year-old pensioner by the name of Gillian Duffy. They spoke at some length whilst television cameras recorded the entire interview. Duffy was clearly upset with the state of the country as well as the state of the Labour Party. She claimed that she had voted Labour her entire life but now she was "ashamed of saying I'm Labour." Brown told her not to be ashamed and explained that they have "improved the health service, financed more neighbourhood policing, we're getting better schools and we're coming through a very difficult world recession." He then added: "You know what my views are. I'm for fairness." Duffy explained how she wanted Labour to return to the three most important issues: "Education, health service and looking after people who are vulnerable." She mentioned that "there are too many people now who aren't vulnerable but they can claim and people who are vulnerable can't." Brown made a mess of answering this point and Duffy interrupted him by adding "You can't say anything about the immigrants... But all these Eastern Europeans what are coming in, where are they flocking from?" Again Brown made a hash of answering this point by giving Duffy a weak statistic off the cuff.

Brown look flustered the entire interview and when he said his goodbyes to Gillian Duffy, he forgot that his microphone was still attached to his lapel. Brown entered his car and spoke about the interview to a member of his team, thinking that he couldn't be heard. Brown called the interview a "disaster" and asked whose idea it was to put Brown with "that woman." He was asked inside the car as they were out of view of the cameras, "What did she say?" Brown replied: "Everything. She's just a sort of bigoted woman that said she used to be Labour, I mean, it's just ridiculous." Brown was absolutely ridiculed for this in the press. And rightly so. Brown naturally thought he was speaking in private, so, if this is how the Prime Minister speaks about his electorate on this occasion caught on microphone, how does he speak about us the rest of the time? Moreover, this was the Prime

Minister. Not some outlandish backbench MP with a mouth. If this is how our leader speaks about us, how do the rest of them describe us?

Brown apologised both publicly and personally to Gillian Duffy. Brown called himself a "penitent sinner" and added "Sometimes you say things that you don't mean to say, sometimes you say things by mistake and sometimes when you say things you want to correct it very quickly." Whilst apologising, Brown projected a smile as if to make light of the whole situation. He obviously wasn't smiling inside and quite clearly wanted the ground to open up and swallow him. Brown's mistake of thinking he was in private lost him huge support in the general election. He was probably going to lose anyway by this time but it added to our national distrust in him, the Labour Party, the government and politicians entirely.

Boris and his 'Johnson'

The Conservative MP for Uxbridge and former Mayor of London, Boris Johnson, is often labelled Britain's most popular politician. However, he isn't that different from the rest of his stereotypical peers. But, in Boris' case, it's his private life that is controversial, as he failed to keep his soldier in his pants. Johnson married his first wife, Allegra Mostyn-Owen, in 1987 only for them to divorce six years later. That same year, Johnson married barrister Marina Wheeler. It was widely reported in the press that Johnson had been having an affair with one of his staff at the *Spectator*, Petronella Wyatt. Johnson immediately dismissed the accusations, calling them an "inverted pyramid of piffle." At the time, Boris was on Michael Howard's front-bench as the Shadow Minister for the Arts. The Conservative leader asked Boris to tell him the truth, if not the press. However, Johnson told Howard the same thing and the leader of the opposition trusted him.

Two days later, it was confirmed that Johnson had indeed been having a long-term love affair with Wyatt and that Wyatt was pregnant. Johnson had reportedly told Wyatt that he would leave his wife for her. Wyatt eventually had an abortion and they mutually ended the affair. Michael Howard sacked Boris for lying to him and, at the time, David Cameron called it "the right thing to do." Johnson's wife, Marina Wheeler, kicked him out of the house for three weeks. This wasn't Johnson's only affair. In all he has had three reported extra-marital affairs and is thought to have fathered a child with Helen Macintyre in 2009. In 2013, many demanded the child have a DNA test to see if Johnson was the father.

Even after the affairs and love-child, Johnson still remains popular. However, to many, he is simply a cross between an old fashioned Etonian Tory and a modern-day celebrity. Although this controversy surrounded his personal life, it was the act of lying to his party leader and to the press that makes this a real issue. We are not to judge politicians' private lives but if revelations occur and they lie about them, how can we trust them as people of their word? Howard made the right decision to sack Johnson from the front bench because he lied directly to his face. His integrity seemed to remain intact though because of his alter-ego as a celebrity. Comparable to any footballer or actor having an affair, Boris didn't seem to be affected by the controversy, still making a joke of the whole situation. It's difficult to suggest that Johnson was in the wrong for having the affair in the first place because it's his private life and he can do what he likes if it doesn't affect the British public. But, if we elect politicians, we want them to be squeaky clean in all areas of their life. And that includes having affairs. Because nobody will vote for a politician who isn't loyal and trustworthy. That is, until you come across the enigma that is Boris.

Chapter Two

Broken System

It wouldn't matter if I voted.

- Lauren, aged 19

Young people these days, especially first-time voters, see the system how it really is. More so than older voters. There's no hiding the fact that our system is a two-horse race fronted by two parties that acknowledge the systematic failure of the entire process, but keep hold of it to promote themselves. It's no mistake that the Greens and the Liberals are often the parties of choice for the minority of young people who actually vote. They realise the frustrating existence of our political system and try to rock the boat by voting differently. For those who choose not to vote, the fault of our system ultimately lays in the archaic and undemocratic first-past-the-post structure. Imagine being – or perhaps you are – a first time voter. You have the choice to vote for any party that you wish. You read the manifestos, watch the debates and decide that you think the Green party best suits you. But then you are told that the Greens simply have no chance of winning the election and it will be between Labour and the Tories. You have three options: Number one, you vote Green anyway and hope that everyone else sticks to their guns. Number two, you decide to tactically vote and switch to Labour to keep the Conservatives out of power. Or number three, you decide to not vote at all because you realise that your vote won't matter in the slightest. Unfortunately, options two and three are the most common, making the entire process a farce and undemocratic. It shouldn't be that our votes don't matter and we shouldn't have to throw our vote away in favour of tactically voting to keep the party we hate the most out of power. The failures of the systems impact greatly on the thoughts of young voters. But the young people who don't care for politics aren't impacted by the failings of either system. And if they are, they're oblivious to the route cause.

Electoral Reform

Out of the 100 young people surveyed, 51 per cent said that the system doesn't work, 31 per cent said they didn't know if the system worked, leaving a mere 18 per cent suggesting that it does. Young people do not feel like their votes matter because whoever you vote for, it's only ever going to be Labour or the Conservatives that get into power due to the first-past-the-post system. It's not just young people that feel this way. The general consensus within the entire voting population is that the first-past-the-post system doesn't work, and the call for proportional representation is widespread. The problem is, the only way we can get a referendum on our voting system is through our elected MPs and any such referendum would be against the interests of the establishment and therefore won't happen internally.

On 5th May 2011, a referendum was held concerning the voting system in the United Kingdom. We were asked, "At present, the UK uses the 'first past the post' system to elect MPs to the House of Commons. Should the 'alternative vote' system be used?" The turnout for the referendum was lower than the turnout for the previous general election in 2010. A sweeping 67.9 per cent voted to stick with the first-past-the-post system and decline the change in how we elect MPs. The *Guardian* put the failure of the alternate-vote referendum down to Nick Clegg. It seems harsh to put the failure on him but they declared that Clegg would be "everybody's second preference" and Clegg became a hate figure for the 'No' campaign. I personally believe that the general public didn't want the AV format because many didn't understand it. The establishment recognised the confusion behind the format and they capitalised on it. To place all the blame on Clegg seems generally harsh. It's widely accepted that alternate voting is more democratic than the first-past-the-post system but Britain rejected the change and remained a less democratic nation.

Although alternative voting is more democratic than first past the post, it's not as democratic as proportional representation. However, because we had the AV referendum in 2011, you get the feeling that the establishment won't declare another referendum on the voting system anytime soon. It's like they've kept this generation 'sweet' with the AV ref and swept the idea of changing the system under the mat. "We gave you referendum in 2011 on the voting system. Why do you want another one?" Because we need proportional representation to democratically represent the country. On the face of it, the first-past-the-post system seems the most democratic, simple and easy form of voting. Whereas systems such as alternate voting and proportional representation are seen as complicated and slated with bad press due to the risk of extremist parties gaining power.

The first-past-the-post system also allows for tactical voting. With the current system, many of the electorate vote for the best-worst candidate. For example, they may have hated Ed Miliband less than David Cameron and therefore would've voted Labour to keep the Conservatives out. The frustrating thing is, both big parties know this is the case, don't want to change it and instead use it for their benefit. In the run-up to the 2015 general election, Conservative MP Nick Boles tweeted: "Ask yourself this. Who does Vladamir Putin want to see running Britain after 7th May?" It's obvious what Boles is getting at here and he used the fact that Ed Miliband comes across as a weaker person that David Cameron. How much truth there is in that is irrelevant. It's a clear example of how the Conservatives use the first-past-the-post system in their favour and try to persuade you into tactically voting for them. This is the general problem with the first-past-the-post system as it always ends up with two main parties. For people that don't know much about politics, telling them that this is how our voting system works often makes them shocked and astonished that this is happening in 21st-century Britain. It's extremely unrepresentative and it's utterly biased.

Karl Marx was Right

The failings of capitalism have been written about for over one hundred and fifty years. The inequality, class struggle and social divide that come with it are its biggest failings. Yet, we are told that capitalism is the best system for our economy and society. It allows everyman to become rich, own more capital and better himself. These are the ideals on which the system is set, but unfortunately, it doesn't work this way. Noam Chomsky would describe it as 'wage-slavery'. This is the idea of being a cog at the bottom of the capitalist machine whilst the oligarchs, CEOs and presidents sit at the top in their mansions, yachts and private jets. He uses this term 'wage-slavery' in the sense that we are paid in meaningless fiat money whilst being the slaves to the powerful who treat us badly and do little work themselves. Slavery was never abolished. The simply pay us now.

But we are told from an early age that this is how life works and that you must abide with everyone else. The clichés you were always told when you were a kid – "there's no such thing as a free lunch" and "you don't get anything for free in this life" – equally reaffirm that the capitalist system is thrown at Western children as a way to keep us in line and maintain the system. Marx believed that people should have the option to live the life of leisure if they so wished. He acknowledged that there is so much wealth that not everyone needs to work and there should be a redistribution of wealth so that this could be made possible. The problem is, the people with the power would be at threat and they are scared of losing their capital. Therefore, the capitalist narrative tells us that people who don't work are lazy scroungers who don't deserve respect. Marx argued that we shouldn't label them as 'unemployed' but instead as 'free'.

Marx argued that capitalists will do anything for profit and that this makes work massively insecure and human beings expendable. If the company can see a way of making more money, they won't care for a second to axe as many workers as it takes. Not only did Marx suggest that work is insecure but that work is also economically unfair for the employees. Marx argued that profit actually meant the theft of talent and hard work from the workers leading to exploitation and further inequality. Capitalism creates an enormous class divide with the people at the bottom never having a chance to get to the top. (Unless one wins the lottery jackpot.) Marx thought that the people at the bottom or the proletariat would come together and rise up against the bourgeoisie, creating a social revolution and smashing the class divide. However, the problem is, Marx saw it as black and white. You're either at the top or at the bottom. Whereas the people saw it a lot more grey. For instance, a lawyer isn't at the top but he certainly would discredit himself from being at the bottom with the coal miners and blacksmiths. Therefore, the system is divided up into more than just two groups and the collective bottom is far too small to start a revolution.

It's the right-wing ideology of capitalism that has made one in five people in Britain live below the poverty line. And it doesn't get much better across the pond where the richest one percent of people in the United States own more wealth than the bottom 90 per cent. It looks like the American Dream didn't work out as planned. At least for 90 per cent of the population it didn't. This is capitalism at its worst. We have the stats, we see the poverty. But they say we can't change it. They won't change it. The problem is, if you start challenging people about the system, they say that you're not living in the real world and tell you that your left-wing ideas will never be reality. The civil rights activist Martin Luther King Jr. said:

> *Capitalism does not permit an even flow of economic resources. With this system, a small privileged few are rich beyond conscience, and almost all others are doomed to be poor at some level. That's the way the system works. And since we know that the system will not change the rules, we are going to have to change the system.*

The reason a failed economic system discourages young people from voting is because they feel like this is it. They don't see themselves thriving under the system and the young adults of today certainly see themselves worse off than their parents were at their age. Mark Fisher argues that capitalism has presented itself as the only realistic political-economic system. Many young people agree and can't see past this. Why would they bother voting for politicians who still support a system that doesn't help them? Young people need an alternative to capitalist dogma because the young are often the poorest in this system.

Young Debt

In March 2015, *BBC Newsbeat* reported that more young people had sought debt advice in the last five years than ever before. The national debt charity StepChange said "four times as many people asked for help over the last five years with more than 40,000 in 2014." This report was written in the middle of the 2015 general election campaign whilst David Cameron and the Conservative Party were arguing that the economy was growing and more people were in work than ever before. As far as Cameron was concerned, he was right. The economy was on the up and more people were working. However, these were just numbers on a report and in real life, the people working and living in the economy were struggling. The numbers may have looked good and made Cameron feel mighty but, to the average person, they didn't translate to more money in their pockets.

It's not just the rise in debt advice that's alarming. Perhaps more so is the rise in usage of food banks and the number of them too. In 2015 there were over 400 food banks across Britain with over 900,000 people frequenting them in 2014. In the 6th wealthiest economy in the world, nearly a million people need charity to eat. Moreover, in 2014, there was an estimated 185,000 homeless people in Britain. That's also with 635,000 empty homes across the country. That's not a working system, is it? A system that says it's working in terms of numbers but doesn't translate surely is a broken system.

Labour and Ed Miliband argued that the numbers were false because of zero-hours contracts. Miliband argued that the rise in these contracts lowered the unemployment rate, but realistically, people may not even have an income on the unpredictable nature of these contracts. Miliband was clutching at straws. Attacking zero-hours contracts was like pointing out that sleeping in a mouldy house is causing a smoker to have trouble breathing. Yes, it's not helping but it's irrelevant when you look at the root cause. In this case, the system is broken and Miliband's comments were pointless and merely a pathetic plea to win votes.

It seriously doesn't help when it doesn't pay to work either. There are many families that are simply better off on benefits than if they worked. Again, a working system would change this. A working system would make sure that working is a means to an end and that it's beneficial to do so. There's something very wrong with a system that says it's working and growing but the citizens don't feel it and often struggle more. A working system would correspond in real terms. When more people are said to be working, they should be able to live without struggling. When the economy is supposedly growing, the average person should have more money in their bank account. It shouldn't be the case that the numbers deceive the general public as for those who don't struggle, they see the statistics and think the system works.

The Scottish Referendum

During the Scottish Referendum campaign, young people all across Scotland embraced politics for the first time in their lives. For this referendum, 16 and 17 year olds were given the opportunity to vote and more than 100,000 turned out to do so. The correlation was quite clear when regarding the entire nation as 84 per cent of the country voted yes or no in the referendum. In fact, it was the biggest turnout at any election since universal suffrage in 1918. There are many reasons why the turnout was so much greater than any other election and I don't think it's as simple as planting all the success on one factor. However, a lot of the Scottish people didn't see this referendum as a political vote. They simply saw it as a question of identity. Meaning, the politics behind the referendum wasn't important. All they cared about was whether they saw themselves as Scottish or British.

It's a question that riles debates all over the country and not just in Scotland. Questions over identity have been asked in all four nations but it goes further than that too. Places such as Cornwall and Yorkshire constantly fight to have their identities heard over being English or British. The identity question gets people talking because we all believe that we have our own individual identities and without them, we may as well not exist. This was felt deeply in Scotland as the idea of being Scottish first and British second is rarely ever seen by outsiders. A clear example of this is Andy Murray and his career of being the 'British Number one'. Therefore, the high turnout can be explained by the referendum not being about politics but rather a question of national identity.

This links in with the second factor of why there was such a huge turnout. The people of Scotland weren't voting for politicians. Moreover, they weren't voting for the Westminster Elite. Yes, the likes of David Cameron, Ed Miliband, Gordon Brown and Alistair Darling all backed the 'No' campaign but this didn't matter to the Scottish people because for once, they weren't conjuring essays of pretentious waffle in order to gain personal votes. I'm not suggesting that the establishment were necessarily trying to keep the United Kingdom together for the people of Scotland, but they weren't simply out to win party seats. Also for the 'Yes' campaign, the people of Scotland had the likes of Nicola Sturgeon and Alex Salmond whom weren't part of the elite and many people felt that they could trust the SNP members if Scotland went independent. It was a chance for many to finally be governed by people that they elected, instead of the Conservatives or Labour.

Thirdly, it was a simple referendum. The electorate were asked "Should Scotland be an independent country?" The ballot paper said "yes" or "no". There wasn't any confusion like the Alternative Vote Referendum in 2011. People turned up knowing what they were voting for and voted easily when confronted with the ballot paper. The end result kept Scotland part of the United Kingdom with 53.3 per cent of the nation voting 'no'. It was a great victory for the 'No' campaign but moreover, it was a great victory for democracy. It showed that the entire nation, including young people, can make decisive choices when given the chance. The thrill of such a big turnout made many wonder if it will impact on the turnout for the general election in 2015 with many speculating that now so many young people of Scotland are registered to vote, they will take up the option of doing it again. And, amazingly, they did. Voter turnout in Scotland was the highest of all four nations and the level of young voters continued with that correlation.

The buzz behind voting in Scotland will make many young people continue doing so but across the border in England and in Wales and Northern Ireland too, young people haven't had an opportunity like the Scottish Referendum to make them connect with politics. The turnout of young people for the 2015 general election was much less in the rest of the United Kingdom than in Scotland for this very reason. Not only has the Scottish Referendum got more young people involved with politics, but it showed that if they thought that their vote mattered, they would vote.

Democracy Under Threat

Democracy in Britain is under threat. Some would even go as far as saying democracy doesn't exist in Britain. Britain joined the EEC in 1973 as a trade agreement and since then, it has grown enormously, becoming the European Union that we have today. It now has its own parliament, politicians, it's own bank, currency and the hope for a European army has been discussed. The European Union now has democratic jurisdiction over the United Kingdom, making it possible for politicians in any of the EU states to vote on laws that might be introduced into Britain. Therefore, politicians who were not voted for by Brits have the power to change the law of Britain. That's not democracy.

We may complain at times about being part of the European Union as it gives us less control but the loss of control means nothing when you actually look at our government. One of the most agreed-on points concerning the British government amongst the majority of the parties, obviously excluding the Conservatives, is the fact that we need to abolish the House of Lords. The majority call it an outdated system with others adding that there's nothing democratic about it. This is a point that Labour, UKIP, the Lib Dems, the Greens, the SNP and Plaid Cymru all agree upon. The House of Lords is made up of men and women who are not elected by us. They are chosen selectively by the Prime Minister or they have inherited the seat through their name. There has been call for the House of Lords to be replaced by an American-style senate with elected members which would be far more democratic than what we currently have with the House of Lords, where members are appointed instead of voted for. We're hardly a beacon of democracy if the body that can veto laws isn't chosen by the electorate. Moreover, the same goes for the royal family. The Queen does have the power, although she's never used it and probably never will, to veto bills passed through the Commons and the Lords. Again, she's a person with power that hasn't been elected. That's simply not democratic. All it does is keeps the fire burning for royalists and traditionalists.

Filibustering: Starring Jacob Rees-Mogg and William Hague

The act of filibustering is seen as a key skill in party politics. The MPs that can filibuster the best are used by their parties to drown out bills that they disagree with. It's said that the best filibuster in the House of Commons is the Conservative MP for North East Somerset, Jacob Rees-Mogg. Rees-Mogg was educated at Eton before going onto Oxford. In January 2012, a debate was held in the Commons regarding the introduction of the Daylight Saving Bill which would have seen the advancement of time by one hour for all or part of the year. The bill was submitted by Conservative MP Rebecca Harris only for her fellow peer to filibuster it. Rees-Mogg argued that his constituency of Somerset should have its own time-zone, 15 minutes behind London, if the bill was passed. This was his way of showing how ridiculous the bill was. As Rees-Mogg held this viewpoint, he filibustered it out of parliament by speaking for the entirety of the allotted time and drowning out the bill's details.

When the Sustainable Livestock Bill was debated in the Commons, Rees-Mogg filibustered that out as he had with the Daylight Saving Bill. Rees-Mogg spoke at great length about the quality of Somerset eggs, the sewage system and the Battle of Agincourt. Rees-Mogg even recited poetry during this debate. He suggested that the poem was from a mug that he used to own when he was a child. It read:

Let the wealthy and great, roll in splendour and state. I envy them not, I declare it. I eat my own lamb, my own chicken and ham. I shear my own fleece and I wear it. I have lawns, I have bowers, I have fruits, I have flowers. The lark is my morning alarmer. So, jolly boys, now let god speed the plough and long life and success to the farmer.

This speech didn't go down well with the opposition and the deputy speaker made it clear that he didn't want to hear poetry in the House of Commons. Rees-Mogg also gained media attention when he used a 29-letter word in the Commons: 'Floccinaucinihilipilification'. This is the action of estimating something as worthless. Rees-Mogg's use of this word is clear evidence of the pitiful nature of filibustering. He used filibustering as a stage for his vocabulary at the price of democracy. It's somewhat ironic that Rees-Mogg has attacked Cameron's administration due to the lack of democracy. The annoying thing is, it's not just Rees-Mogg that practices the act of filibustering. The former leader of the Conservative Party, William Hague, declared that he once drafted a 24-hour speech to play his role in government as a filibuster. It's frustrating that parliament works like this. How can something so immature and pathetic be allowed to happen? More evidence that the system is broken in more ways than one.

You Never Listen

If the system really worked, it would benefit the people. Moreover, the voices of the people would be listened to. This clearly doesn't happen. Under the Blair administration, over one million people signed a petition not to go to war with Iraq. A further three million people lined the streets in protest. However, Blair and his government (not forgetting he was backed by the Conservatives) ignored the wishes of the people and entered an illegal war with Iraq. A working democratic system would've seen the protests and held a referendum for the people to decide whether we went to war with Iraq. The Blair administration ignored the people campaigning, the people who signed the petitions and the opposing MPs from minor parties.

It's estimated that 500,000 people are avid watchers of the reality TV show *The Only Way is Essex*. Double the number of people signed the Iraq War petition and six times as many people marched on the streets in protest of the war. If the bosses at ITV didn't think *TOWIE* had a big enough audience, they wouldn't keep producing the show. To them, 500,000 people constitutes a loud enough voice. But, for the British government, three million is nothing. The voices of three million people were dismissed like a bad smell under the Blair administration but they still expected them to vote.

A lot of young people were amongst the protestors against the Iraq War. If they're ignored so instantaneously, no wonder it puts so many of them off politics. If over three million people take to the streets in protest, surely they can't be ignored in a working democracy. And yet, MPs will forever explain how democratic our nation is and they tell us that we should count ourselves as lucky. Yes, we are fortunate not to live in a state like North Korea or Uganda but it's not enough. They want us to settle for second best because we're in a better situation than dictatorships and regimes across the World.

The Blair government should've listened to the people on this matter and if they did, perhaps thousands of civilians and soldiers wouldn't have been killed, the Chilcot Inquiry wouldn't have been needed, saving millions of pounds, and the government wouldn't have lost so much trust from the British electorate. Yes, the United States probably would've still entered Iraq, killed thousands of civilians and executed Saddam Hussein, but our government would have held its head up high.

Unfortunately, we are now in a position where Blair and his cabinet are being looked into for illegal war crimes and the British population have a deep sense of hatred towards politicians as they feel they don't listen to them. If the system worked, I don't see how three million voices could go unnoticed on such a colossal matter. They can't expect people to vote for them if they can see for themselves that the system is broken. There simply should've been a referendum on the matter. It should have been truly democratic, and the politicians should have made the choice of reforming the system.

The Ability to Hold MPs to Account

The ability to hold members of parliament accountable isn't currently existent. If an MP fails to deliver points on their manifesto or is involved in something dodgy, the electorate of that specific MP's constituency have no powers to remove them from their office or call a by-election. Therefore, once you elect an MP, you don't have the power to change this during their five-year term. Yes, the leader of the MP's party can discipline them and they have the power to remove them from their post. (Usually they are politely asked to resign. They wouldn't risk the controversy of firing them as they'd think it'd damage the party.) When an MP does resign, a by-election is called and the electorate finally get to choose a new candidate.

However, shouldn't the people be able to choose when the MP has to go? If an MP was caught evading tax through an offshore bank account and the electorate of their constituency didn't approve, they should be able to kick them out. Moreover, if an MP fails to deliver a vital manifesto promise, the electorate should be able to remove them from office. UKIP, once again, have jumped on this by suggesting that if 20 per cent of the electorate sign a petition in eight weeks, the MP should be recalled and a by-election should take place. People are attracted to this because it puts the power in the hands of the people. Unfortunately, I can see this backfiring as many MP's don't win by 81 per cent and over 20 per cent already want them out of the job before they've been voted in. This could end up with by-elections being held every week. Nevertheless, it's a start to system reformation with power being devolved back to us and making us a more democratic nation. It'd also make sure MPs stay squeaky clean and stay away from dodgy deals as they'd need to in order to stay in a job. You see it all the time: candidates promising unrealistic and utopian policies just to gain votes. If the electorate had the power to hold MPs accountable, they'd be more incline to follow politics. Not just because they can kick them out when they've done something wrong but because politicians would have to think twice about behaving badly.

A working system would already have something like this in place. A device that allows us to hold MPs accountable. A working system would allow us to kick MPs out for not following through with promises. Imagine if such a device was in place and Nick Clegg was recalled for not following through on his tuition fees promise. Under the UKIP policy, it's almost inevitable that over 20 per cent would've signed a petition to recall Clegg. (Unfairly, as I've previously discussed.) My personal view is that it would be unfair but if there's a big enough objection, he should be held accountable. It links back to the Iraq War protests and getting the government to listen to the people. The electorate are choosing a person to represent them and if they feel that the elected MP has crossed lines, they should be recalled.

Typical Career Politicians

Our political system allows for men and women to live a life of politics, never have a job outside of Westminster and hold constituency seats for as long as they like. Not only that, the British electorate choose candidates to represent them and the lucky elected few get a salary that is nearly three times the British average. Many MPs hold the same constituency seat for over twenty years. Conservative MP Kenneth Clarke, for example, has held his constituency seat in Rushcliffe since 1970. Clarke's Tory peer Peter Tapsell was the MP for Louth and Horncastle from 1966 to 2015 and before that he held the constancy seat of Nottingham West for five years. There's nothing in place in our system to stop MPs from holding seats for that long. If people vote them in, they can stay as long as they live. In fact if you are the longest serving MP in the House of Commons, you are known as the Father of the House, as Peter Tapsell was until 2015 when he decided enough was enough. If it wasn't for her own party forcing her out, Margaret Thatcher would have tried to stay as Conservative leader for as long as her health would have allowed her. Some politicians know when to stop as Tony Blair did when he made way for Gordon Brown in 2007. David Cameron announced before the 2015 general election that if he won the election, he would've stepped down after the second term. Most politicians aren't like this though. Career politicians are far too many these days. Many have never held a job outside of Whitehall and many only assumed power due to their wealthy backgrounds and family influence.

This has been a talking point for some years. In 2013, the *Telegraph* reported that Tony Blair called Ed Miliband a "career politician." They wrote "Tony Blair took a swipe at modern MPs like Ed Miliband for lacking experience outside politics, claiming they should work normal jobs for several years before heading to Westminster." Blair said following careers in other areas before taking up politics was vital as it meant the MPs were "better able to see the World." It's not just Ed Miliband that fits in this category either. His brother David Miliband along with David Cameron and George Osbourne can all be defined as career politicians. (Or were, in David Miliband's case.) Blair was right that there are too many career politicians and the general consensus is that Blair was also right when he said politicians should have jobs before they enter politics. The electorate do not agree that politicians can take one foot in Westminster and never leave. A working system wouldn't allow for such conservatism. Change is always needed in any area of life. It helps freshen things up and makes things more progressive. Perhaps if there were less career politicians and more real people in politics who have held other jobs for years before hand, people would be more inclined to support them.

Chapter Three

Disinterest, Disillusionment
& Obliviousness

Politics doesn't interest me because it's boring
- Jamie, aged 18

Disinterest, disillusionment and obliviousness are, without doubt, the three biggest reasons why my peers don't go to the polling station and cast a vote into the ballot box. In 21st-century Britain, most young people do not like politics. It's dull, boring and really not cool. The mentality of young people has changed dramatically in the last few years. In fact, I'd say the change in mentality came under the overview of Tony Blair. With the rise of New Labour came the extraordinary growth in connectivity and instant technology. For children, going out to play football or climbing trees were becoming archaic pastimes. Growing up, my generation would much prefer a PlayStation to a bike. As these children grew up in the boom of Blair, their mentalities continued to change and their thumbs became the most used parts of their bodies.

Now that the children of Blair are the 18 to 24 demographic, they show utter obliviousness to politics as if it doesn't exist. Many have become so used to living in front of a screen that they have missed the political train as they begin their journeys. Now, they stay inside and scroll through Twitter whilst watching *TOWIE* or playing on the Xbox or PlayStation. Politics is irrelevant to their lives because it doesn't affect the things that they interact with on a daily basis. If, for an evening, they do put down their controllers or turn off Netflix, they imitate *Geordie Shore* by necking a bottle of WKD whilst taking a selfie. Why would men in dull suits, passing boring legislation, appeal to them when they're having such a great time getting drunk and interacting with their friends? I'm under no illusion that teenage drinking is new – it has been prominent in youth culture since the 50s – but it's the combination of this, the rapid advancement in technology and the hereditary political apathy that causes a cocktail of obliviousness towards politics. Yes, voting takes five minutes to do, so surely they can take the time to put down the Absinth and vote? This point is irrelevant because why would they want to do this? It's not fun. It's not cool.

Being a young person in 21st-century Britain isn't the same as being a young person in Thatcher's Britain or even Major's premiership. You could ask every young person in the country to state their hobbies and interests like one would on a CV. I would firmly suggest that 70 per cent of them wouldn't be able to get past the words football, films and music before wondering if it would be acceptable to put socialising, drinking or gaming as an answer. Life as a young person in 21st-century Britain is strange. You have to be on social media and you have to like drinking. Other than that, it's sport or reality television. Politics doesn't fit in anymore. It's not seen as cool to be an activist against corruption. It's not seen as cool to join a young political rebellious group anymore. Young peoples' role models are equally as disengaged with politics, with most of them being stars of reality television, pop or YouTube. Times change and the previous engagement with young people in politics is quickly diminishing.

The lack of representation across the board hasn't helped either. How can anyone expect young people to pay attention when all they see is the same white old face every time they see a story about politics? Those young people that do enjoy politics and are actively engaged with it are seen as boring and uncool. The mentality of the Blair era has made young people think they're all James Dean. As if they all firmly know what is acceptable and what isn't. It's the coolness of something that makes young people partake or stay far away from it. Especially in the age of instant mass spreading of pictures and stories. It's made young people fearful of doing anything differently as they'd instantly be spoken about on Facebook or Twitter. Because politics is no longer normal amongst young people, it would be seen as straying from the socially acceptable. You're not allowed to miss a Champions League group match to watch a political documentary. That just wouldn't be cool and you'd instantly be victimised on social media. There's almost an imaginary wall of what is cool and what isn't. If you jump the wall by watching *Question Time*, you're not cool. Young people do not care for politics because it is jumping that wall. It's not socially acceptable to join a youth wing of a party or discuss it on Facebook. This mentality has driven down the young vote since the rapid advancement in technology and it will continue to do so until something drastic happens.

There's a real problem amongst young people in this country when it comes to politics. If there wasn't, I wouldn't be in a position to write this book. The British youth simply do not care for or do not like politics. Some find it distressingly boring and others don't even remember that it exists. Out of the 100 young people that I surveyed, 59 per cent answer 'no' to the question "Does politics interest you?"

Does Politics Interest You?

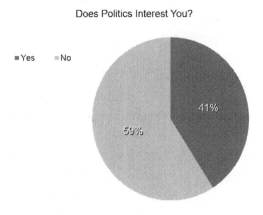

However, when they were asked "Does Politics Affect your Life?", 65 per cent answered 'yes' with only 24 per cent saying 'no' and 11 per cent stating that they didn't know. So, if young people realise politics does affect them but are still disengaged with the subject, the answer must be politics itself. The problem doesn't lay with the youth and we're too quick to moan at them because they don't take an interest. The youth don't have a problem; politics does.

From Stalin to Mr Bean

One would assume politicians making a job out of the process and having a laugh would make young people more inclined to engage with the process. However, it seems to have the opposite effect on them. During a speech about the armed forces in the House of Commons at Prime Minister's Questions, the Liberal Democrat, Vince Cable, made a joke out of the former Prime Minister Gordon Brown. Cable said: "The House has noticed the Prime Minister's remarkable transformation in the last few weeks from Stalin to Mr Bean. Creating chaos out of order rather than order out of chaos." The Commons subsequently roared with laughter. Cable basked in the hysterics like a successful amateur stand-up comedian at the Edinburgh Festival. Yes, Cable's joke did lead up to a very poignant remark about the armed forces but, for a respected MP and in a historic, sensible and serious place of work, his delivery was childish to say the least.

He's not the only politician to try and bring laughter into the House. David Cameron also made a joke in the Commons, directed at the former Shadow Chancellor, Ed Balls. The Labour MP made a gesture with his hand and Cameron responded: "We've got a new hand gesture from the Shadow Chancellor. I would've thought that after today's briefing in the papers, the hand gesture for the Shadow Chancellor should be bye bye."

Cameron then finished off the insult by saying "You don't need it to be Christmas, to know when you're sitting next to a Turkey." The Commons turned into a mosh-pit of laughter and even the Speaker, John Bercow, failed to control the house as he was laughing with the rest of his peers. This wasn't a one-off from Cameron either. After a question in PMQs about bingo, David Cameron suggested that Ed Miliband enjoys a game of bingo because "it's the only time he ever gets close to number 10."

There's no denying Cameron's delivery of a put-down but, should the Prime Minister, or any MP for that matter, make a joke in the House of Commons? Surely it should be a place of serious debates as these are the people running the country. In November 2014, Conservative MP Penny Mordaunt slipped the word 'cock' into her speech several times as part of a dare. In fact, she said 'cock' six times in total and the entire speech was laced with innuendos. Mordant admitted that her dare was given to her by her colleagues in the Royal Navy as a forfeit for a misdemeanour. If Mordaunt was attempting to put the House and the political process into disrepute, I'd have admired her. However, the MP for Portsmouth is a classic Tory politician and any such attempt isn't her style. As she admitted, this stunt was merely a dare, which put her in very bad stead. She, like Cameron, Cable and many others, are simply showing to the electorate that they aren't taking the job seriously. An unfair point, they would argue in return, as I'm sure behind the scenes they work tremendously hard to deploy their policies. However, we don't see behind the scenes. All that we see is politicians making jokes and laughing at each other on a Wednesday afternoon in Prime Minister's Questions. And, if they aren't taking that seriously, how can they expect us to take them seriously?

PMQs

Prime Minister's Questions is a ridiculously pathetic pantomime.

Even David Cameron himself suggested that it was the worst part of the job and if he had his way, he'd get rid of it. But, Cameron also hypocritically suggested that it was a good thing to have because it holds the Prime Minister accountable and makes him clear on his policies. I'm not too sure a childish exchange is firstly the best way to hold the Prime Minister accountable nor should the Prime Minister need such a facade to be up-to-date with his government policies. As far as I'm aware, nobody believes that Prime Minister's Questions is a good thing. It's not the fact that MPs are questioning the Prime Minister that is pointless. It's the childish behaviour. If that stopped and PMQs became a serious platform for grilling the Prime Minister and holding a substantial debate, it would hold much more substance than it does now. The pathetic jokes, point-scoring and put-downs make a mockery of British politics. I'm surprised Ed Balls hasn't made a 'yo mama' joke as of yet. It really is a pathetic showcase for all involved.

Even when the jokes and put-downs have stopped, you're still left with middle-aged men and women making a tsunami of unrecognisable noise. Nobody can talk over the undefinable racket and the speaker has less control than a referee at an ice hockey match. Once you look past the childish nature of PMQs, you're left with MPs asking the Prime Minister questions that more often than not are from his own backbench and have been chosen by the party's whip. This means, before PMQs, the whip has informed the Prime Minister's backbenchers on what to ask him so that he looks good in front of the television cameras. If all the questions were negative, the Prime Minister would crumble and the party would suffer enormously. So, the questions are ultimately bogus, the answers are staged, the participants made noises like wild animals and the front benches throw insults at each other like a school playground.

Prime Minister's Questions isn't needed in our political system and it needs to be replaced by something that gets an end result. It's almost like they're keeping it for two reasons: Firstly tradition, but secondly and more plausibly because if we get rid of PMQs and replace it with something that really holds the Prime Minister and his party to account, they'd run scared and do everything they could to protect the deceased event. It's not in their political interest to replace it. Even Labour would keep it, because if they were in power, the Labour prime minister would want to keep it in his interest just as much as a Tory prime minister. PMQs is one of the main reasons why young people don't vote. They see this pantomime and are instantly turned off by the whole process. Young people see voting as quite a mature thing to do but then they see politicians acting like children in PMQs.

Party Politics

The phrase 'party politics' is one of the main things that puts people off voting. Although more common with the two main parties, it is something that all politicians do, even if they suggest that they don't. UKIP's Nigel Farage has made it aware that he dislikes the game between Labour and the Tories but he himself has played the same game. Just, when Farage does it, firstly he plays it against all of the other parties and secondly, he's forgiven because he's seen as the man of the people simply stating what the electorate are apparently thinking. Now, the former Labour leader Ed Miliband could say the same thing, but because he's of Labour ilk, he's seen as playing party politics. Even the Greens do it despite the fact that Natalie Bennett has said how she's fed-up with the point-scoring between Labour and the Tories. Usually when the Greens insult another party, it's UKIP on their immigration policies, as Plaid Cymru have also done. The SNP make digs at Labour for the fight in Scotland and they attack the Tories across the border out of sheer antagonism. Nick Clegg and his Liberal Democrats question Conservative policy but still go into coalition with them. But, the smaller parties fly under the radar because of the utter scale that Labour and the Conservatives play party politics.

Before the 2015 general election, the Labour MP for Denton and Reddish, Andrew Gwynne, tweeted "It's 23 years ago to the day – Thursday 9th April 1992 – that the Conservatives last actually won a General Election." What was Gwynne trying to do here but play party politics? Maps like Gwynne care more about getting one over the Tories than serving their constituency. It's like teenagers having a spat in the classroom about a football team not winning a trophy for 20 years. It's childish, pointless and utterly pathetic. The electorate do not care about party track records in winning elections. They care for the current election only and who is the best candidate.

Party politics always raises its head on BBC's *Question Time*. Naturally, they always have a Labour and a Conservative representative on the panel. When either are asked a question about their policies, they will always answer by slating the opposition's alternative in order to score points and get one over the opposing party. You often get politicians defending their admiration for their own parties with some even stating 'love' for them. Referring back to the football analogy, party politics is nothing more than supporting a football team. They get irate when you criticise their party, they attack other parties for bad track records and they slate the leaders of the opposition all for self-admiration. The electorate hate party politics. The feebleness and pithy nature turns most people off voting for them. It irritates everyone that watches political debates or interviews when they can't help but get one over another party. First-time voters won't get into politics if they see politicians caring more about point-scoring than policy.

The Complete Lack of Choice

It's amazing that the parties can even point-score against each other when they're all so similar in the first place. You can see this when you compare their 2015 general election manifestos. Below is a table of ten policies that the election was fought over.

	Conservatives	Labour	Lib Dems	UKIP	Green Party	SNP	Plaid Cymru
EU Referendum	✓	X	X	✓	✓	X	X
Leave the EU	X	X	X	✓	X	X	X
Cut Immigration	✓	✓	✓	✓	X	X	X
Ban Zero-Hours Contracts	X	✓	X	✓	✓	✓	✓
Lower Voting Age	X	✓	✓	X	✓	✓	✓
Reform the Voting System	X	X	✓	✓	✓	✓	✓
Introduce a Living Wage	X	✓	X	X	✓	✓	✓
Cut Tuition Fees	X	✓	✓	X	✓	✓	✓
Abolish Trident	X	X	X	X	✓	✓	✓
Welfare Cuts	✓	✓	✓	✓	X	X	X

From the table above, you can clearly see that the only party that wanted to leave the European Union was UKIP. Agreed that three parties promised European Referendums but supposedly when the referendums happened, only one party would be campaigning to leave. Concerning immigration, only the progressive Greens, SNP and Plaid Cymru didn't want to decrease it, giving the electorate of England only one main party that held this policy. What if you lived in England, didn't want to cut immigration but didn't want to vote Green? The only party in England that wanted to end austerity was the Greens giving simply not enough choice to the electorate. Again, what if you lived in England, wanted to end austerity but didn't want to vote Green? The lack of choice is frankly disgusting. Especially the similarities between Labour and the Conservatives when they're the only parties that can get into power with our failed first-past-the-post system. They agreed on half of the above points.

Nicola Sturgeon summed it up well when Ed Miliband stated that there was a difference between David Cameron and himself. She said: "I didn't say there wasn't a difference between you and David Cameron. I said there wasn't a big enough difference." She pointed this out on the BBC debate on 16th April. The reason she said this was clear. As the leader of the SNP, she wanted to play the role of a 'king-maker'. She wanted to see the back of the Tories but didn't want to enter into a coalition with a Labour government that quite clearly agrees with the Tories on most issues. I would agree that there is a clear divide between the progressive parties and the other four. However, that simply isn't enough choice as the Greens only field candidates in England and Wales, and Plaid Cymru and the SNP naturally only field candidates in their respective nations. Therefore, at a push in Wales, there's only a maximum of two progressives to vote for and in England and Scotland, merely the solitary candidate. One may argue that the Liberal Democrats sway to a progressive nature but I think if you have to argue over that fact, they clearly aren't of that ilk. If you take a look at the political spectrum with the main seven parties placed, you can see that there isn't enough choice and just how similar they really are.

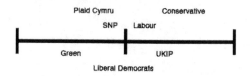

Naturally, many would argue over the positions of the parties on the political spectrum above, not least the positioning of Labour as being right-wing under Ed Miliband. Ahead of the 2015 general election, it was asked whether the problem with Labour is that they are too left-wing. Many, including myself, argued that Labour were actually more right-wing than under Blair. That was their problem. Labour were meant to be this utopian socialist party of the working class but as far as I could see, they'd ditched these routes under Blair and have only gone further by distancing themselves from the unions. Yes, their policies may be directed at ordinary people, but there's nothing socialist about them. No matter how you rearrange it to fit your thinking of the parties, they'll all still be clumped together, not giving the electorate enough choice. And it's that lack of choice that doesn't make the electorate interested enough to choose one. If they're all so similar, they can't equally represent the entire nation, can they? Young people are usually more inclined to the left but if the furthest left are the Greens (a party that people realise can't win the election) they're just not going to bother voting at all. If the party furthest left was a party capable of winning the election, more young people would turnout.

The Stereotypical Politician

Not only are all their policies pretty similar, the politicians themselves are incredibly alike. As Nigel Farage likes to point out, only 7 per cent of the country went to public school but it is that seven per cent that rules over us. A report in the *Guardian* in August 2014 showed that it's the seven per cent that are taking the majority of power in Britain. According to the report, 50 per cent of the House of Lords went to public school. This is probably not as surprising as the stats suggest as people are tuned in to the fact that the House of Lords is naturally a playground for the retired elite. That number drops however, when you enter the Commons where 33 per cent of the House were public-schooled. It's no majority, but it doesn't truly represent Britain. Surely for fair representation, only seven per cent of MPs should be public-schooled politicians.

It only gets worse when you see that 24 per cent of MPs went to Oxford or Cambridge. Moreover, the majority of the most influential figures in British politics were all privately educated. David Cameron, George Osbourne and Boris Johnson all went to Eton and then Oxford. Ed Miliband and Ed Balls also attended Oxford with Nick Clegg attending Cambridge. In fact, 59 per cent of the Conservative cabinet between 2010 and 2015 went to Oxbridge and 33 per cent of the shadow cabinet did so too. Not only is this an unfair representation of Britain but it also shows why we hold this perception that all politicians are so similar.

The most influential politicians and the men with all the power are completely different to the general public. There are no similarities between us and them. They dress the same as each other, style their hair the same, talk the same and use the same hand gestures. Incidentally, they're hand gestures that only politicians make. No ordinary person would wave their hands around like Cameron and Osbourne do. Two weeks before the 2015 general election, Nick Clegg's Twitter profile picture came under fire as he was wearing a North Face jacket. Nothing surprising about a middle-aged man sporting clothes from North Face but because Clegg is a politician, he was slated and even accused by some of "following gangster fashion." I'm not sure how 'gangster' North Face is, but because Clegg actually had something in common with the general public, he was slated. The problem is, Clegg wants to be seen as a normal guy when he's quite simply not. He's as Oxbridge as the rest of them and his sporting of a fashionable brand made some feel awkward for his attempt at being normal.

We're all aware that politicians are sometimes told what to say and what to do. It's the fact that they have to be told how to act because they don't know how to be normal that is the disengaging part. Miliband is so Oxbridge that he can't eat a bacon sandwich and Cameron used a knife and fork in order not to show himself up in the same manner as Miliband. Yes, Farage likes a pint in his local but he can't shake off the public-school image that easily. Especially as he wears more tweed than the rest of the Commons put together.

The Obvious Lack of Equal Representation

This lack of representation doesn't stop at where they were schooled. The stereotypical politician is a straight white male of about 45 years old. Prior to the 2015 general election, there were a total of 191 female MPs whereas there were 459 male MPs. Out of the 191 female MPs, 99 of them were Labour, 68 were Tory and 20 were SNP. In 2010, only 21.1 per cent of candidates running in the general election were women. In 2015, that number had increased but only to 26.1 per cent. Although generally the number of women in politics had increased, it is still completely unrepresentative of Britain.

Most of the parties are trying to change this by fielding more female candidates and trying to engage young women in the subject of politics, but you almost get the impression that they're not doing for fair representation or equality. Perhaps the motive is to prove a point or even to quieten some feminist corners. We do live in a country (and this isn't just relevant in Britain as America is much the same if not worse) where we assume women's suffrage has ended and both genders are equal. At least, that's how the media likes to portray it. Women aren't represented equally in most areas of life and the glass ceiling is very much still a thing. This mentality seems to have taken over us because of Thatcher. We assume that because we've had a female prime minister, we're all equal. But we're not – as female representation in the Commons shows.

It's even worse for youth representation. After the results of the 2010 general election, the average age of the House of Commons was 50. The youngest ever MP was 21. In fact, there have been nine 21-year-old MPs since 1880. That changed, however, in 2015 when the SNP candidate Mhairi Black attempted to make history as the youngest ever MP at the age of 20. She was duly elected, but exciting as it is, her presence isn't enough. She is the only 18 to 24 year old in the Commons after she won her constituency seat of Paisley and Renfrewshire South. The youngest MP is referred to as the Baby of the House. It's hardly fair that middle-aged men can see themselves in Nigel Farage, down the pub, drinking a pint, but an 18-year-old hasn't the same connectivity with an MP. Every voting age group is represented in the Commons but for the 18 to 24 year olds. I understand that people would have quarrels about inexperienced politicians, but I'm utterly sure that there are young men and women who could run the country better than David Cameron or George Osbourne.

Another area of immense lack of representation in the House of Commons is with ethnic minorities. After 2010, there were a total of 27 MPs with ethnic-minority backgrounds. This meant only 4.2 per cent of MPs were ethnic minorities. After the 2015 general election, 27 more black, Asian and ethnic-minority MPs were elected. The 2011 census showed that 12.9 per cent of the UK population are ethnic minorities. This is yet again another piece of evidence to show how poorly the House of Commons is represented. You only have to look at the leaders of the parties at the 2015 general election to see this. Cameron, Clegg, Miliband, Bennett, Wood and Sturgeon are all white. That's one of the reasons why Obama did so well in the two general elections in the States. He won support from the ethnic minorities to defeat the Republicans. The Hispanic community especially was deeply supportive of his campaign. With further representation of people of difference races, eventually one of the main parties will have a non-white leader. At the moment, we label all young voters as having the same reasons for not voting, but young people of different races do not have somebody to vote for because they don't connect to any of the white politicians. They honestly can't suggest that they have much in common with young black people or know how young Asian women are feeling.

There are currently only 32 openly gay elected members of parliament. The first was the former Labour MP Maureen Colquhoun in the late 1970s. The most recent was Daniel Kawczynski who came out as being bisexual in 2013. There have only ever been two gay members of the House of Lords: Lord Alli and Baroness Stedman-Scott. There has never been a transgender member of parliament or lord. However, Nikki Sinclaire, formerly of UKIP, was the first transgender member of the European Parliament. It's clear that representation of the LGBT community is very, very scarce indeed. Although we live in a country of legal gay marriage, the LGBT community still come across many men and women who don't think gay people should have even had this right. A *YouGov* poll in 2013 showed that 37 per cent of people opposed same-sex marriage. If over 30 per cent of people didn't think the LGBT community deserved equal rights here, how can we be sure this many people wouldn't vote for a gay candidate in an election? In April 2015, the *Huffington Post* reported a story about the UKIP candidate for Wallasey, Geoffrey Caton, who called gay people "arse bandits" on his Facebook profile back in 2013. He also posted a picture depicting homosexuality as a 'sin'. Canton denied being homophobic even though these images were publicly seen. The LGBT youth community need to see more gay and transgender members of parliament who actually represent them.

MTV Generation

Disinterest doesn't always have to stem from something, and in the case of politics, this seems to be the case with young people and I guess with a lot of older people too. Politics isn't a subject that is liked by people across the board. It's not like football or films where the disapproving minority really are miniature.

Politics doesn't have elements that entice huge groups of young people to get involved. Instead, it sits on the back shelf or, more often than not, it sits in the trash, as the majority of young people don't even think about it. There isn't anything about politics that draws young people in. After all, why would an 18-year-old girl want to watch *Question Time* when she could be watching something she enjoys like *Made in Chelsea*? There isn't the glitz and glamour of shows like the *X Factor* that draws young minds in. This isn't something you can change. I'm not suggesting we dress Nick Clegg up in a sequined dress and make him perform with fireworks going off and a crowd encouraging him.

Politics is the way it is because it's actually meant to be serious. Young minds aren't instantly drawn to seriousness as they're meant to be living their lives in an alcoholic coma under a lorry on some lay-by near Milton Keynes. At least, that's the subconscious narrative that young people are given. Politics isn't seen as a 'cool' thing to do. What's cool about knowing who the shadow minister for transport is? Politics is naturally grey, dull and boring because it's important. Running the country isn't meant to be a catwalk show full of good-looking, fashionable people who are all sleeping with each other like an MTV reality show. And, it's not just about young people not seeing it as cool. Westminster doesn't reflect the lives of young people. *The Only Way is Essex* reflects their lives. *Geordie Shore* reflects their lives. *Newsnight* reflects their dads' life. Young people won't take an interest if they don't see it in their subconscious narratives. Politics is boring to young people as much as *TOWIE* is boring to a 75-year-old from the Cotswolds.

The last Saturday before the 2015 general election was prominent in the year's social calendar. Moreover, it was prominent to every sports fan across the world. Floyd Mayweather and Manny Pacquiao took to the boxing ring as millions of Brits stayed up to watch the duel of the century. The fight started just before 5:00 am GMT. This was the most hyped event of the sporting calendar and, to many, it was an event that meant more to them than anything else. Now, fast forward to the following Thursday, election day. The fate of the country was to be announced in similarly early hours as the 'MayPac' fight. However, far fewer people stayed up to watch the results come in than watched the fight. Why? Exciting as an election can be, it's not something millions of people can be bothered to deprive themselves from sleep for. The hype of the fight urged people to put matchsticks between their eyelids like young children in 1969 staying up to watch the moon landing.

Even though the election results hold far more importance and dictate the way we live, a boxing match between two men from outside of Britain attracted far more of an audience than the election results. Moreover, the proportion of young people that stayed up for the boxing was far more than those that watched the election results. It's not the fault of politicians or the system for that matter. Politics should be dull and grey as a matter of importance. We shouldn't attempt to make it cool (as many politicians and campaigners already have) because it won't change anything. Seriousness and importance aren't wanted in the majority of young peoples' lives. Having a good time and enjoying one's youth is far easier. I'm not implying that it's too important for young people but that they don't want importance over a bottle of Jägermeister and a playlist of house tracks. I'm also not implying that it's a lost cause because there are things that can be done, which I will come to in a later chapter. However, we'll never bypass the fact that Whitehall is dull, traditional and dull. These are facts as much as something can be called a fact.

Where are All of the Role Models?

It seems odd to suggest that young people need role models in order to get involved in politics. But, if the disinterest is very much apparent, role models may be the only key to getting young people interested. If a 19-year-old girl, who has no interest in politics and finds it utterly boring, sees her favourite singer or personality actively involved in politics, she might be influenced into following her idol into politics. The celebrities that young people admire and look up to hold more influence than their parents or friends. Their actions are very much copied by their followers, be it how they dress, their social life or their stance on an equality matter like the *HeForShe* campaign backed by Emma Watson of *Harry Potter* fame.

Going back to Russell Brand, his recent political activism has invited so many disinterested people into politics. Now, many will argue that Brand is nothing but a hindrance to the cause but I completely disagree. The people Brand has attracted have either never voted before – in which case Brand's message not to vote is has no relevance towards them – or they are already polit-ically minded and have completely changed their views but, importantly, still vote. Brand has got people talking. His influence isn't just on young people either. Non-voters of all ages have declared their support for the Essex comedian. Brand has got people into politics who had never thought about it before because he portrays a different way of seeing the political game. His left-wing messages have given people something different to follow whereas previously, you were either right-wing or centre.

Brand has debated with another celebrity on the matter of voting. The lead guitarist of Queen, Brian May, a prominent Green Party supporter, has suggested that Brand's message has a negative effect on young people. May is actively trying to get people into politics and his support for animal rights has gained him and the Green Party some support from the youth. At a Q&A hosted by Brand after the launch of his new film *The Emperor's New Clothes*, May asked "If you really don't want to vote and you don't want us to vote, what do you want us to do to achieve the things that we know we need to do?" Brand naturally answered in his extravagant way but May wasn't having any of it.

Another pop star who has declared her distaste in Brand's message is Paloma Faith. Unlike May, she is very much a trending celebrity and her influence is possibly more poignant that May's due to her fan base. Faith has been trying to actively engage her fans by using Owen Jones as her warm-up act during her tour. Faith hopes that Jones' can help engage her young fans with politics. In an interview with *Channel 4 News* in March 2015, Faith said "I think Russell Brand is wrong. I do think it was irresponsible, because I think what he did was play more into the hands of power again because the powerful always vote – it's in their interest to vote." She then went on to say how the music industry is "scared" of politics but it's clear that Faith isn't. What Paloma Faith does is what we need more of. Her audience is naturally younger women who probably don't have an interest in politics. Faith can break down the barriers of youth and politics and rebuild a bridge to make young people vote. There are a few celebrities such as Michael Sheen, Martin Freeman and David Tennant who all actively support parties and get involved with their campaigning. Unfortunately all of these men don't have a massive following with the youth and it's people like Paloma Faith, who have this following, that need to come out and spread the message of the importance of politics.

There's No Incentive

If, like many young people think, voting doesn't matter because politicians make false promises and don't follow through with their pledges, there really isn't an incentive to vote. As I've already said in the first chapter, young people don't trust politicians and this gives further reasoning to the lack of incentive to vote. What do young people get out of voting if politicians aren't going to stick to their promises? Moreover, there is a point that politicians know that young people are less likely to vote and, therefore, don't cater for their needs in terms of party policy. This can be said for the Conservatives the most, as they more than any other ignore the youth vote and focus on the older age demographics. Moreover, in April 2015, David Cameron announced that if they regained power, they would stop housing benefit for people between the ages of 18 and 21. This policy backs up the point that they do not care to attract the youth vote.

This is partly why the young people that do vote tend to tick the box of Labour, the Lib Dems or the Greens as they certainly do focus on the youth. This is also down to the mentality of the youth though, as many young people have left-wing ideas and see capitalism as evil. So, perhaps the Tories have also caught onto this which is why they don't cater for the youth as much as any other demographic. Returning to Nick Clegg's tuition fee promise in 2010, many young people saw this as a chance to get involved in politics because they finally had an incentive. Finally a party was catering for the young and promising radical change in the form of university fees. However, Clegg's broken pledge may have destroyed the political minds of an entire generation.

Russell Brand argued this on his YouTube channel *The Trews*. He said that Clegg had "annihilated political faith in a generation of young people." Perhaps Brand is right there. Clegg gave a generation of young people a reason to vote, but when he achieved power, he broke his promise and the thousands of young voters that voted for him have now become disinterested in the entire show. Even when parties accommodate for the youth vote, this generation won't have an incentive because they realise that politicians break promises left, right and centre. For example, during the 2015 general election, the Greens announced that they wanted to cut tuition fees as the Lib Dems pledged. Labour also promised to cut tuition fees by £3,000 in hope that they could secure more of the youth vote. However, a different party making similar pledges which were broken before won't make young people interested in voting as they'll believe that the promise will be broken again.

There is also reason to suggest that if young people thought that politics affected their lives, they would have an incentive even if parties aren't catering for them. But, take Cameron's premiership between 2010 and 2015. The economy was in recovery, fewer people were unemployed, thousands of jobs had been created, and yet the average Jack on the street wasn't feeling any of the apparent 'trickle-down effect'. It's no wonder the youth don't believe that politics affects them because in many respects it doesn't. An incentive wouldn't necessarily get every young person voting but, it would certainly boost political activism amongst young people as they'd campaign for better motivations to vote.

Chapter Four

Lack of Knowledge

I don't understand politics. That's why I don't vote.
- Asif, aged 23

Not understanding something that you are asked to form an opinion on is a recipe for disaster. Moreover, if that opinion then impacts on the future of the country, it's perhaps understandable that those in this position choose not to vote. This lack of understanding does frustrate many young people as they actually want to know about politics in order to cast a legitimate vote instead of being told who to vote for by a friend or family member. I would suggest that those who do not vote due to not understanding politics would in fact like to be informed about the subject. However, there are young people that do not understand politics and don't care that they don't have an understanding.

I asked 100 young people, "Do you understand politics? e.g. Do you know enough to vote?" 41.41 per cent answered 'No'. I would go as far to suggest that this lack of understanding applies beyond young people and you would see a trend in the other demographics. Not understanding the basics of politics is enough to put anyone off voting. Not understanding the fundamentals can make people miscalculate their votes. The problem of lack of knowledge is a risk to democracy and Western society. It stops revolutionaries and idealists from introducing new ideas into the political system and transforming the political make-up of the country. If the quest is to get people to vote even though they don't understand the policies, parties or ideologies, then fine. But, if the real mission is to get people engaged in the subject in order to form ideas of their own to then implement when voting, I would argue this lack of knowledge goes further than young people that don't vote. And that is dangerous. Not having knowledge makes one more probable to be convinced by party propaganda and personal slurs. Those in this position are then more likely to be persuaded to vote for a party that doesn't necessarily represent them. It is this that is undemocratic. It helps enforce the broken political system and boosts votes for the two major parties as they are the ones with enough money to use for propaganda and hate campaigns. This is exactly what the Tories did at the 2015 general election. For the entire campaign, they slated Ed Miliband and declared that the country would fall apart under his leadership with huge stock piles of crippling debt and an even bigger deficit.

As a disenfranchised nation, I'm not surprised by the number of young people that don't understand politics. I'm not surprised that many don't understand the subjective political spectrum or simply don't know how to cast their vote. The lack of clear direction and education is directly a result of the disengaged Thatcher generation not giving their children the knowledge to vote as well as the insufficient teaching of the subject at school. When I asked my 100 respondents "Which of the following best describes why you don't vote?", 18 of the candidates replied with the answer "I don't know enough to vote." This was the third largest choice after "I don't trust politicians" (22) and "other" (23). There is a clear problem here. There is a proportion of young people that don't turn out to vote because they don't understand certain aspects of the subject or merely how to go about it.

I'm sure that naturally the 18 to 24 year olds that voted in the 2015 general election will gain some understanding by 2020 as they grow older and politics becomes relevant or even interesting to them. And it's that point that proves not understanding isn't the main reason why young people don't vote. If one doesn't have an interest in something in the first place, they won't understand it. There's not a cell in my brain that takes an interest in equestrian so when I see horses dancing at the Olympic Games, I'm ultimately confused as I don't have a clue what's going on. It's the lack of interest that makes me not understand what it takes to win a gold medal on the back of a frolicking pony and the same applies to young people and politics. If they don't originally hold any such liking for the subject, they simply won't understand what's going on. Yes, schools could do far more to get them engaged in the first place and a good teacher should be able to give students an understanding of subjects that they don't like. But for those that haven't had any education and aren't interested, politics remains a black hole of knowledge.

I did a simple search on *Twitter* on election day to see if people were talking about the fact that schools should teach politics. There were endless tweets from young people saying this exact point. One young man Tweeted: "They should teach politics and about the different parties and their policies in Citizenship or RE at school." Many seemed to be in the position of knowledge whereas others declared they didn't understand politics because of a lack of education. However, I'm not entirely convinced myself that not understanding the subject is the ultimate reason why young people don't vote as, if that's the only thing stopping you from voting, surely putting your hand in your pocket, withdrawing your phone and doing a bit of research would clear any confusion you may have. I am convinced, though, that there is a proportion of young non-voters that don't understand politics and don't care enough to do the minimal research when they could be watching endless Vines of cute pug videos or scrolling through their Tinder matches. There's a difference between not wanting to vote and not understanding enough to vote. The act of crossing a box for a candidate is universally known. But it's the frightening, daunting and confusing prospect of turning up at the polling station and not knowing where to go once you're through the door. This does impact on young peoples' decision whether to vote or not, as I don't believe a proportion of 'Blair's children' would put themselves through the anxiety of the event for something that they hold very little or no interest in.

Miss, What Does VAT Mean?

The reason for this lack of knowledge stems from school. Politics as a subject isn't taught in schools; at least if it is, it's not on the national curriculum and it's only in a handful of private establishments. (Already creating a class divide.) Most pupils at senior/high schools know little or nothing about politics which doesn't put teenagers in good standing when it comes to voting. At most schools, there will be an election for the president or head boy/girl. They will be chosen by the pupils after each person casts their vote. This is the only form of politics that teenagers are introduced to. Although it's a start, it really doesn't do anything to teach teenagers about policies, parties, political history or even how parliament works.

Teenagers then have the right to vote at 18 and don't have a fragment of knowledge about the process. I have personally been asked questions by my peers about politics. Simple questions that one would assume wouldn't be asked. Schools are leaving it up to the pupils themselves to learn about politics and they're simply not doing this. After all, what average 15 year old wants to learn about parliamentary processes or electoral reform? You'd be hard pressed to get them to watch the 'Iron Lady' in their spare time.

Once they leave school, politics then can become an option at A-Level. However, in the most deprived areas, and even the not-so-deprived, it won't be an option. Even at my average comprehensive, politics wasn't on the cards. Most young people have to wait until university to learn about politics but the students that do go on to do politics already have an interest and have taught themselves about the subject already. Most young people won't engage with politics until they reach the second or third demographic. Meaning the voice of the young is being lost because of lack of knowledge and that is not how democracy should work.

We can't blame the youth for not understanding politics enough to vote. The education system should be teaching them the fundamentals and giving them a voice instead of leaving it up to them to learn about something their grandparents enjoy. Democracy should be a subject in the textbooks of every high-school student. It's as crucial to our knowledge as history and geography and yet it is overlooked for some unforeseen reason. Not only does this mean young people aren't being taught vital information but it encourages the class war and social divide that enwrap our country. Young people from privileged backgrounds are being sent to schools that teach them about politics, giving them a head start from an early age. I'm not suggesting politics is slapped onto the national curriculum but encouraging schools across the country to teach pupils about politics in already-existent Citizenship lessons would be far more beneficial than a school election for class president. Young people have the infra-structure to be taught about politics, more so than any other demographic. It should be utilised and encouraged.

What Do the Different Parties Stand For?

Many young people do actually want to engage with politics but, as discussed, they don't know anything about the parties or what their policies are. This makes it extremely difficult for them to differentiate between the parties and construct a view in order to vote. It's naturally a massive turn-off for young people as they struggle to make a clear choice in an election. Although at the 2015 general election the BBC website collated all of the policies from each party and had them in one simple place, a lot of young voters argue that there isn't a clear platform to find out which party stands for what policies. Yes, there are websites that do hold this information such as the BBC but, in an age where parties attack each other with misquotes, propaganda and smear campaigns, the policies get merged into one and many forget or lose track of what each party stands for.

At the 2015 election, UKIP's immigration and European Union stance was widely known and yet, when asked, many would suggest that UKIP were in favour of deporting already migrated Europeans. Some even suggested that UKIP wanted a total ban on immigration by cutting off the borders. The Greens were also suggested to have said that it shouldn't be illegal to support terrorists groups such as ISIS or the IRA. Natalie Bennett reputedly denied these remarks and suggested that she was misquoted when talking about Nelson Mandela and the ANC. It's times such as these that help confuse the electorate and merge policies and lies into one giant political mess.

It doesn't help much either when all of the parties look and sound the same. If a white man in a suit suggests tuition fees should increase, that could've been any one of four of the main parties at the 2015 general election. Not only does this lead to misrepresentation but it also reaffirms the failures of the first-past-the-post electoral system as many confused voters choose to vote for one of the two major parties out of lack of understanding of the smaller parties.

There has been an increase of online tools enabling voters to digest what the parties stand for and also which parties they most connect with. These online surveys ask the user a series of questions about key social issues with a multiple choice format that includes the policies of each party on the respective topic. These tools were backed enormously by the Green Party during the 2015 general election campaign as it came to light that a vast majority of users that took the survey connected with the Green Party more than any other. There are platforms out there that help engage and educate voters prior to elections but I would argue that there aren't any during the other four and a half years of parliament when there isn't a general election going on. During this period, voters can get lost and policies change like managers for Chelsea. Politics is forgotten during parliament and it's only when an election creeps up that these platforms are introduced and advertised.

How Do I Vote?

The voting method in England is old-fashioned, manual but ultimately simple and effective. However, even though it's straight-forward enough to cast a vote, a substantial number of young people don't know how to do it and it effectively puts them off making the trip to the polling station on election day. Voting for the first time is confusing for everyone as it's a brand new experience but the helpfulness of the civil servants conducting the polling station makes all of that confusion disappear. In an age where anxiety amongst young people has never been greater, the uncertainty about a new experience is stressfully off-putting. It's alright to say everyone was in that position at some point and it didn't put them off before; however, because of the rise of anxiety amongst youngsters, experiences such as this aren't greatly accepted.

The increase in anxiety has generally been put down to the unsociable nature of modern childhoods with many children neglecting in-person contact and opting for speaking to people in front of a screen or behind a headset. Moreover, the rise in anxiety has also been linked with the paralleled introduction of sexting and cyber-bullying. A *BBC Newsbeat* article suggested that there has been a "rise of nearly 50 per cent in four years of 12 to 17-year-olds admitted for serious depressive order, anxiety disorder and stress-related issues." There's no denying the fact that mental health issues are a direct result of the rapid growth of social technology with the popularity of Twitter, Facebook, Snapchat, Instagram, Tumblr and previously Bebo and instant messenger platform MSN in the early noughties. Never before have young people been the subject of more social pressures than now and, with the need to conform and be as good as celebrities on social media, the stress of society increases the levels of anxiety and in many cases depression. Mental health problems have always been around but they weren't previously brought about by something so apparent. If the average 18-year-old girl from Chester is struggling to conform and is constantly bullied by trolls online, who they know in person, that young woman's levels of anxiety will skyrocket. She's not going to want to experience something that is stressful at the best of times. Although the method is perfectly simple and all it takes is to turn up, say your name and cross a box, for many young people suffering mental health problems this is far too much.

As I declared previously, the method of voting is practiced frequently at schools across the country when class presidents, head boys/girls and prefects are elected. Although this rightly teaches young people how to cast a vote, it does not show young people the process of where to go at the polling station and it is this that young people find discouraging enough not to turn up. I agree that this is no reason not to cast your vote but it is nevertheless a reason for many young people. I myself know peers who declared that they didn't know how to vote. They didn't know where to go or what to do. In an age of smart phones in every pocket and handbag, our voting system is still manual in every sense of the word. You firstly have to go to the polling station, use a piece of paper to cast your vote and then the votes are counted by hand. It's not surprising that 'Blair's children' find it confusing when they've lived their entire lives in front of a keyboard. It's like asking a ten year-old to set the VCR to record *Emmerdale*. Although as it is the voting system is universal, it certainly has failed to keep up with the rapid growth of technology and those that live in a digital world.

How Does Parliament Work?

As well as the systematic method of voting being out-of-date, British parliament itself is also denying revolution. The last major reform in the Palace of Westminster was in 1918 as universal suffrage became a thing with the introduction of votes for women. The building itself is crumbling and falling apart and the parliamentary procedures are as ancient as the decaying structure. Although I have already spoken about the need for reform at Westminster, I haven't addressed the issue that many young people simply don't know how parliament works. Many can't describe the difference between the two houses or they don't even know there are two separate bodies. The fundamental workings of British government aren't known by a majority of young people which makes one wonder why not. Again, there is the issue of lack of education, but it must be more than that.

The complexity might be an issue. Why are there two houses? What's a backbencher? Who are the opposition? What does the speaker do? Because of the archaic language used, there can't be surprise to hear that this is why young people don't know how our government functions. There isn't really a necessity here in order to choose a candidate to vote for. But, it must be off-putting to be told to vote for a candidate without knowing firstly what they'll be doing in parliament once elected and secondly, how the process of what they'll be doing works. Simple terms such as 'bill' are often unknown to young voters as never have they used it out of the context of paying for a meal. Although I see the fastidiousness and selective nature of this point, there's no denying that most young people wouldn't have a clue how their local MP can pass a bill about double-yellow lines outside of their local primary school. And, I'm sure there are a number of young people that can describe inertly how the Commons works but they are probably voters and have an interest in politics. The other fifty per cent of young people that do not vote almost certainly wouldn't be able to describe such a process.

I'm not entirely sure the workings of parliament are excruciatingly complex but I do believe they are complicated enough to put off outsiders who hold little or no interest. Similarly the offside rule in football can be judged this way. It itself isn't complex at all and is known by 99 per cent of football fans. However, those who dislike or don't really take an interest in the beautiful game will struggle indefinitely to understand the simplicity of the rule, thus putting them off the entire sport. Although the struggle to understand the offside rule is much more well-known than parliamentary process, let it be said that both are equally as difficult to understand for an outsider. Although reform is badly needed inside Whitehall, much more needs to be done about educating not just young people but everyone about the inner workings of the houses in order to give more reason to vote. The more knowledge non-voters have about what they are voting candidates in to do, the more likely they are to make their way to the polling station.

What is the Political Spectrum?

The political spectrum is, at the best of times, a complex, ambitious and subjective felicity. There's no definitive right or wrong answer with parties and individuals placing themselves on the spectrum differently to how everyone else perceives them. The subjectiveness of the spectrum makes it extremely difficult for political new-comers to decide which party best represents them. Moreover, the simple existence of such a spectrum is unknown or vague to most. The birth of New Labour in the mid-90s altered the spectrum completely as Blair, Brown, Campbell, Prescott and Mandelson took Labour past the Liberal Democrats and hugging the cold arm of the Tories. Blair declared himself to be right-wing and his policies certainly backed his declaration with the selling of public services, the need for foreign conflict and the shrinking of the state. It was but Labour's lacklustre need to borrow from the banks that made them slightly less right-wing that Thatcher's Britain. However, Blair and his blue Labour comrades still attracted the support of the working class and of the left. The political spectrum was no longer linear as the party was practicing capitalism better than the Tories but the party still had strong working-class connections.

The spectrum, in some people's eyes, is still far from straight-forward. Labour, as I stated in a previous chapter, tried to be left-wing under Miliband but came across more right than Cameron's government. With the rise of UKIP, the working class finally had a new party. However, unlike Old Labour, UKIP were firmly right-wing which altered the spectrum even further. Moreover, a vast number of UKIP members and senior figures are former Conservative supporters that have defected due to the Tories' stance on the European Union. So, what we now have is former Labour voters voting for former Conservative politicians, but it's key to remember that a Labour politician would seldom be seen defecting to UKIP. Therefore, we have left-wing voters choosing a right-wing party containing candidates of their former enemies.

As Tariq Ali states in his book *The Extreme Centre*, "we live in a country without opposition." Ali's opinion is that Labour and the Tories are huddled around the Liberal Democrats on a political spectrum so tight, it looks like one party. Although I agree that there isn't opposition, I disagree that Labour were left-wing under Miliband. During the Labour party leadership campaign, Shadow Business Secretary Chuka Ummuna called himself "blue Labour." He certainly didn't want to bring Labour back to the left and his Blairite stance was used to try and win the support of middle-England again after the devastating loss at the 2015 general election.

The political spectrum is a mess as we currently stand. The left is almost non-existent and the right contains the two biggest parties fighting against the third biggest, UKIP, who are also right-wing. It used to be far simpler to deviate between the parties and place them on the political spectrum. But today, it's not only the young that are having trouble with it. It's confusing the entire country with none of the parties really declaring themselves for what they are. It's not as simple as capitalists on the right and socialists on the left anymore as every major party in Britain is capitalist with the slight exception of the Greens. (And even then, their policies simply continue the capitalist system with injections of eco-socialism.)

What is a Council House?

If young people don't understand what they're voting for, why should they make the trek to the polling station in the first place? Moreover, this attitude isn't just common amongst the youth. Things such as tax are often the most misunderstood amongst the other demographics too as there are so many different forms with income tax, capital gains tax, council tax, inheritance tax, corporation tax, national insurance and so on. During the 2015 general election campaign, Ed Miliband and the Labour party tried to promote the mansion tax as one of the main points of their manifesto. Miliband proposed that the mansion tax would help fund the crisis in the NHS and would only affect houses worth over £2 million. However, many voters didn't know this. People with expensive houses worth £800,000 were worried that the mansion tax would affect them. The Labour MP for Dulwich and West Norwood, Tessa Jowell, was interviewed after the election on *LBC* and stated that this was something she was asked time and time again whilst she was campaigning on the doorsteps.

At the same time as Labour were promoting the mansion tax, UKIP were demoting the 'Barnett formula'. This is the amount of money given to each nation in the United Kingdom. It works out better for Scotland and Northern Ireland as they receive over

£2,000 more per head of population than England and Wales. Farage and UKIP argued that the Barnett formula was unfair on the English and Welsh and that Scotland received far too much money. However, whenever Farage mentioned this the electorate often didn't understand how the Barnett formula works and slated Farage insisting that he was only out to help the English. If the Barnett formula was explained properly, the British electorate wouldn't have rejected UKIP's policy so drastically. Moreover, if Labour's mansion tax was properly explained by Miliband and his fellow members, perhaps it wouldn't have turned off so many undecided or leaning Labour voters.

The Liberal Democrats also fielded a policy that the electorate couldn't get their heads around and that was the rent-to-buy scheme thought up by their former leader Nick Clegg. The scheme stated that every time the renter paid their monthly rent, they would gain and eventually increase their stake in the property with the potential right to buy and own at the end. However, this was as complicated as a labyrinth with the electorate wondering how this could possibly work.

The Greens also had policies of confusion with their stance on the constitution. Natalie Bennett announced that the Greens wanted a constitution for the 21st century by starting with a blank piece of paper. However, many didn't perceive this as it was intended. This was a policy of radical reform not one of drab political manoeuvres. Many didn't understand how such a policy could be implemented and quite rightly as Bennett never declared how it could be done. This left many voters unsure of the crazy idea and turned many off. If voters don't initially understand the policies themselves, why would any of them want to vote? If they're not explained properly and taken apart bit by bit in order to give clear and concise understanding, the electorate won't bother turning up on election day and, this is far more poignant for young people as they haven't had years and years of political experience to understand half of the policies.

Politics Doesn't Affect Me... or Does It?

"Politics doesn't affect me." A phase muttered by many of the young non-voters. But are they right? Or, do they simply not understand how it can affect them? I realise the patronising manner of the question but it must be asked. I'm sure there are thousands of non-voters that truly believe that politics doesn't affect their lives and they have intrinsic understanding regarding the subject. But, for some, they state that politics doesn't affect them for reasons of not understanding how it actually can.

In 2010, the Liberal Democrats announced in their manifesto and throughout the campaign that they would abolish university tuition fees whilst the Conservatives were hinting at increasing them and Labour didn't want to touch them. For an 18 year old still at college and about to enter the life of a university student, these policies would have directly affected them massively. Arguably more so than most policies in all three of the manifestos. Young people would have naturally voted for the Liberal Democrats regarding this policy and although many felt that their votes didn't matter after the eventual outcome, the policies themselves clearly affected them as tuition fees were raised to £9,000 per year once Cameron became Prime Minister.

Not every young person goes to university and if they're like me and went directly into full-time employment, the national minimum wage would have been the single most important point in an election. During the 2015 general election campaign, there was lots of talk about a 'living wage' of over £9.00 an hour. Labour wanted to introduce a scaled-down version of this at £8.00, the Greens wanted to overachieve with a £10.00 minimum wage by 2020 and the Tories would increase the minimum wage in parallel with inflation, interest rates and the cost of living. It's hard to understand how many young people don't see how politics can affect them if something such as the minimum wage would directly control their income.

This mentality is understandable when people under the age of 18 are asked if they like politics as they can't vote for any of the policies in the first place. However, once one is of voting age, this mentality is ridiculous. There's obviously a misunderstanding in the minds of young people as politics quite clearly affects every voter. One could argue that it doesn't matter who you vote for because they're all the same but that's different to suggesting that the policies themselves don't affect you. There are members of other demographics where this mentality is visible and again I would argue that this is down to a misunderstanding of the policies. Every demographic has matters that are addressed by politics whether that be pensions, welfare, maternity leave or tuition fees. (Yes, some are better catered to than others due to the parties knowing that older people are more likely to vote than the young.) To suggest that politics doesn't affect you is ridiculous, but nevertheless, there are a number of young people that don't vote because they don't understand how it can affect them.

Put Aside the Rhetoric, Put Aside the Rhetoric and Put Aside the Rhetoric

In an interview with Damon Green for ITV, BBC and Sky News in 2011, Ed Miliband confused his audience and Green himself by continually answering with the same statement to every question that was asked. The interview was regarding the union strikes of July 2011. Miliband's initial statement about the strikes seemed scripted but ultimately normal. He said "The strikes are wrong at a time when negotiations are still going on but parents and the public have been let down by both sides because the government has acted in a reckless and provocative manner. After today's disruption, I urge both sides to put aside the rhetoric, get around the negotiating table and stop it happening again."

Green didn't see anything abnormal about his answer and then asked Miliband "I listened to your speech in Wrexham, you talked about the Labour Party being a movement. A lot of people in that movement are the people who are on that strike today and they'll be looking at you and thinking you're describing these strikes as wrong. Why aren't you giving us more leadership as the leader of the Labour movement?" Miliband's answer caused everyone watching to have deja vu. He replied by saying "At a time when negations are still going on, I do believe these strikes are wrong. And that's why I say, both sides should, after today's disruption, get around the negotiating table, put aside the rhetoric and sort the problem out. Because the public and parents have been let down by both sides. The government's acted in a reckless and provocative manner." Miliband simply rearranged the words in his first answer and repeated himself. Moreover, the answer wasn't even relevant to the question.

And it didn't stop there. Miliband used the same answer five times in total, leaving Green publicly ranting about the interview. He went to Twitter to vent his anger where he accused Miliband of "professional discourtesy." The Miliband interview was one of the strangest interviews in modern political history and went viral as a result. It's obvious that Miliband was told to toe the party line and stick to the script but he took it too literally. If Green was doing a 'Paxman' and repeating the question and Miliband was in turn, repeating his answer, it would be understandable but the questions were clear and completely different. Miliband's answer was irrelevant to every question.

The arrogance from Miliband to show Green zero respect and to make the interview a sham was outrageous. It lost him support and reaffirmed that politicians use language that confuses the electorate and, in this case, do so purposely and unashamedly. Understanding the technical language that many politicians use can be hard and for people that rarely visit the world of politics, it can be overwhelming during a general election. The politicians know this and purposely continue with the rhetoric. Then when you get interviews like Miliband's, it becomes the straw that breaks the camel's back. The young will not vote for people that they can't understand.

Chapter Five

And the Winner of *The X Factor* 2015 is...

The 2015 general election result surprised everyone apart from the Conservatives. Whilst we studied the poll of polls and expected a hung parliament, the Tories were looking at their own private polling and foresaw a winning majority. David Cameron and his Etonian tribe stated their certainty about winning a majority on every debate, radio interview and newspaper column. The battling politicians including Nick Clegg, Nigel Farage and Nicola Sturgeon all denied the prospect of a Conservative win and gave the electorate reasons to vote for the smaller parties as they would inevitably be the king-makers of the election. Even the interviewers and studio audiences laughed when a Conservative spokesperson stated their intention to win a majority. Comparably, Labour also declared their intention to win the election but you got the feeling that they were only saying it because the Tories did and suggesting anything other than a win would come across as negative to the electorate. If, like the rest of us, Labour were reading the poll of polls or the half dozen or so individual polls, they clearly wouldn't have expected a Labour majority but a hung parliament in their favour. After the exit poll, many remained faithful to the poll of polls and rubbished the findings that the Tories were going to win an outright majority. (Paddy Ashdown most prominently.) Then, as predicted by the Conservatives, they won a majority and Cameron remained in power.

I started writing this book just before the campaign kicked off, and throughout, I heard people all around my home town of Gloucester debating about politics. But it wasn't just older people, I heard every demographic give their opinion. The surprising thing was, a lot of young people were talking about politics. Some of the time they were really engaged and there was a buzz in their conversations. However, you won't be surprised to hear that the majority of young people debating about politics held negative views and weren't going to vote. The debates would usually start with a politically active voice and eventually be drowned out by three or four non-voters. One may argue that at least they're talking about it, but they may as well not have been. Their arguments often declared that politicians are all the same, or that they really didn't care about the election. Although this may sound ironic, what this shows is that they were actually engaged with politics as they used their time to talk about it. There's a clear statement here from young people that they do want to be involved and to vote. But there are so many factors that are stopping them from voting that they hold this view of disliking the subject. If these young people didn't care about politics, their alienation wouldn't be expressed. If it was a subject that genuinely didn't matter to them such as ballet for instance, they wouldn't tell us about their hatred and apathy for politics or politicians.

In contrast, the debates between older demographics were embroiling and open-minded. There was so much to discuss during the campaign with the rise of UKIP and the Green surge giving more people a real choice. I didn't consider this election, as many did, to be dull and flat. I thought the variety of television debates brought an added flair to the process and involved the electorate much more. Young people had their own formats with BBC's *Free Speech* and Sky News' *Stand Up And Be Counted*. Both allowed young voters to challenge politicians on policies but, as I stated previously, the participants in the audiences were people already interested in politics. Nobody would sit in the audience of *Free Speech* for an hour whilst their peers sat around them questioning Ed Miliband if they weren't interested in politics or the election. So, although the broad-casters tried to get young people more engaged, all they were

doing was giving the already engaged youth a chance to inter-
rogate politicians for the purpose of good television.

When I announced that I was writing this book, everyone
seemed to give me their two pence and tell me in less than a
sentence why young people don't vote. They thought it was as
simple as that and the reasoning was obvious. What I have
proved is that there isn't one reason why young people don't vote
and you can't, like most things, cast a fishing net over them all
and collectively say why young people don't vote. For some, the
reasoning is complex and thought over, but for others, it's simple
and not given a second thought. It's this issue of treating all
young people the same that has become fashionable since the rise
of New Labour and the birth of the 'chav'. The elderly fear the
youth. Perhaps not as much as they did in the early noughties but
certainly more than the nineties or before. Most sane people will
cross the road and continue walking on the other side of the
pavement if they see an oncoming group of youngsters, due to
fear and complete misunderstanding of youth culture brought
about by the media. Young people have been frustratingly collectivised as a group of thugs and detached from real life. This
problem of labelling everyone under the age of 25 as the same has
spread into every feature of life to the extent that we think young
people don't vote because they ultimately don't care. This is true
for a minority but for others, it's not the reason.

We say that politicians are all the same. But really we know
they're not. You get some amazing politicians that do tremendous
work for their local constituencies and others that stand strong on
the back benches when the rest of their party is formally against
them. On the other hand, you do get some awfully crooked and
corrupt politicians that are simply only in the game for
themselves. It is these politicians that give them a collective bad
name and they are the ones that the media likes to spotlight.
Unfortunately, because of the power of the press and now the
enhanced power they have through social media, corruption is

never far away from anyone's timeline or news feed. And, it's not simply the media influencing young people into believing that all politicians are lying cheats; it's also the parents' negative influence upon their minds. Together, it has put off a large proportion of young people from voting.

I will suggest though, that a lot of young people take this stance because it's what they've been told to think about politicians and politics in general. I wouldn't be surprised if those in this position haven't done a great deal of research or even thought about voting. The propaganda that has influenced their minds has destroyed democracy nearly as much as the system has itself. As we now believe that politicians are worse than estate agents, fewer of us will go out to the polling station to act upon our democratic right. I have presented more evidence than I would have possibly liked to in suggesting politicians are crooked and, unfortunately, I haven't even scratched the surface. That would suggest that politicians actually are as bad as we believe them to be and perhaps when young people don't vote because of this, they should be respected for choosing that stance. It is not respectful however, to hold this stance but not to have sufficient evidence to back it up and to merely go along with the collective idea. Really, that's not the reason they don't vote. If they cared about voting, they would do their homework and see firsthand how 'bad' politicians are. As they don't, it's almost as if they're just saying this as a reason so they're not hounded for not voting. But for those that actually don't vote because they believe politicians are liars and cheats, I really do not believe that this is the main reason why young people don't vote collectively.

Neither do I believe that young people don't vote because the system doesn't work. We all know that the system is broken. Both electorally and socially. You only have to look at the 2015 general election to see how badly broken the electoral system is. For every Conservative MP elected, it took 34 thousand votes.

For every UKIP MP elected, it took 3.8 million votes. Moreover, UKIP had more votes than SNP and the Liberal Democrats combined and yet they won 63 less seats. Twelve per cent of the electorate voted for UKIP making them the third most popular party with voters, but in the Commons, they stand as the joint 10th largest party. Not only is it astonishing that this can happen in a supposedly democratic system, but it also does turn many people off from voting as they simply do not see the point because their vote won't matter. After the election, there was a huge outcry for an electoral referendum and a coalition force of parties signed a petition to get it into Number 10. Although I believe that this does put some young people off from voting, it is not the main reason why. The majority of young people that hold this belief would genuinely be interested in politics in the first place and that is a smaller number than young people who aren't interested in the subject. Therefore, this simply cannot be the main reason why so many young people don't vote. And, for those that aren't interested, this is also something that they would have heard or seen on their social-media timelines, giving them a reason to suggest to others why they choose not to vote.

There is a great deal of misunderstanding and simple unknowingness amongst the electorate and especially young people. It may seem pretentious and arrogant of me to suggest this but it really is a problem. For those who don't have a 365-days-a-year political interest, understanding every policy, outcome or ideological belief will be extremely hard. And for young people especially, who are less likely to have this daily interest, it makes it a lot harder to understand everything. Just overhearing simple debates about the 2015 general election, you sensed that a lot of people don't really understand the subject. I'm not talking about who the right person is to vote for or what each party will supposedly do when they get in such as the Tories destroying the NHS or Labour borrowing money. (Both speculative things that are always debated.) I'm talking about simple things about who can win an election. I heard many on numerous occasions suggesting that UKIP were going to win and Farage was going to be the next Prime Minister. That is a systematic impossibility due to the first-past-the-post system, but they really didn't know this. I'm not sure whether this is entirely people's fault or the lack of education available. I do not, however, believe that most young people choose not to vote because they don't understand politics. Yes, there are some for whom this is the reason. But, the majority, if interested in the first place, would do their research and learn about the subject. Therefore the main reason why young people don't vote is because they aren't interested.

I did previously say that it was wrong to collectively suggest that young people don't care, but that's different from not being interested. Not caring is political apathy. Having apathy would suggest that they are actually interested but are tired of politicians or party politics. Not being interested in the route subject is wholly different. Today, we have access to the whole of history, the thoughts of every human being on the planet, the collectivised work of every book ever written, millions and millions of videos, trillions of images, every song ever performed, every painting ever canvased, every film ever produced, the ability to see any place in the world. All of this in our pockets. Politics just doesn't break the surface of young people's interest anymore with access to so much information. We must not forget that it is 'Blair's children' that grew up with this. They, and I, haven't lived in a world without this. It's not some apathetic arrogant stance that young people take. There's just so much more available to young people that it means politics won't register until they've finished exploring this hive of information. Yes, sometimes this information is a compilation video of fat people falling over or the musical works of Iggy Azalea but that's how it is. Unfortunately I do not think this trend of young people continuing to be the worst demographic in terms of turnout will see much improvement in our lifetimes. But there are some things that can be done to slightly improve the outlook.

Chapter Six

How to Solve a Problem like Eton

There are so many ways to get young people interested, engaged and ultimately voting. But, what we currently have is a government that doesn't seem to care or even perhaps want this to happen. Therefore, getting any substantial change through public institutions such as schools will be difficult to implement. It will be private companies and charities that will fundamentally introduce the biggest changes as they will have intentions to do so. Public institutions run by the government will not introduce basic changes as this is against their self-interest.

Tackling the Key Issue of 'Blair's Children'

Solving a problem that was created unconsciously is very difficult. There's no quick fix for this either. As technology continues to rapidly advance, further generations of young people will get more and more entrenched with technology, and politics will continue to be put on the top shelf. Understanding why young people prefer technology over politics isn't difficult. When you grow up with something, side by side, developing in parallel, you will instantly be at ease with it. Due to the capacity of the World Wide Web, young people have become ingrained within the helix of the internet and it has blocked out anything that doesn't embrace it. Politics needs to be revolutionised in order to fit the trend and look like an interesting felicity when compared with the rest of the 21st century.

It doesn't have to be incredibly high-tech with space-age technology. I'm not calling for the House of Commons to be transformed into a spaceship from *2001: A Space Odyssey*. But technology does need to play a bigger role in and outside of the

Palace of Westminster. The simple abolishment of the archaic voting system within the Commons and introducing a digital system would be a fantastic place to start. It would kickstart the technological revolution that went on whilst the Commons slept. This would get the ball rolling and encourage other parts of politics to embrace technology and engage 'Blair's children' with voting and politics in general.

The problem is actually just distraction. 'Blair's children' are too busy, too preoccupied with social media, Netflix and gaming to see that politics is actually interesting and that it affects everyone. One could compare the sharp rise in technology with the rapid growth of football and its following amongst the youth. Yes, football has always been popular with young people. But, since the late nineties, football has entered a rapid spiral of growth never seen on the pitch before. That is down to technology. Unlike politics, football embraced technology. Therefore, it stayed with the young through Blair's premiership which saw this incredible growth in football whilst politics faded out and has continued to ever since.

Admittedly the comparison is vague but the general thought is very much real. Technology is what young people are comfortable with. It's what they know, what they've always known. Because politics hasn't embraced the digital age, it has escaped the path that young people walk. Perhaps 'Blair's children' are lost and they'll never vote. But I'd like to think that introducing technology would discourage their apathy. However, we need to start again. 'Cameron's children' will soon be able to vote and most will choose not to. We need to tackle this head-on and revitalise politics, bringing it into the 21st century by means of digitalisation.

Bite The Ballot

There are already companies that are trying to get young people interested in politics. One of those charities is Bite The Ballot. Set up in Dartford in April 2010 by David Hughesman and Michael Sani, the charity intended to rebrand politics so that it would interest young people and get them talking about democracy. Hughesman and Sani both took the scheme around schools and colleges and got young people involved in political debates, games and discussions. As the company grew and gained a lot of media interest, they teamed up with ITV News and Twitter in November 2014 and hosted a succession of interviews with the leaders of major political parties in a series called 'Leaders Live'. Nigel Farage, Ed Miliband, Natalie Bennett and Nick Clegg all took part in the interviews. However, David Cameron refused to take part.

The organisation has attracted numerous famous faces to promote the cause. Musician Tinie Tempah, television presenter Rick Edwards and magician Ben Hanlin have all been involved. They even held a national voter registration day where they encouraged people to register en masse. The Bite The Ballot website declares that "during the week of 2nd – 8th February 2015, a world-record breaking 441,500 people registered to vote, including 166,000 on NVRD alone (5 February). This makes NVRD 2015 the most successful voter registration campaign, ever." The website also states that "over 500,000 people have registered to vote because of Bite The Ballot."

The success of Bite The Ballot is very pleasing. Its effectiveness is nothing but a blueprint for more organisations to follow suit and help educate young people around the country. The reason Bite The Ballot works is because they go into schools and colleges and educate the students about politics but putting it in such a way that makes it sound interesting and worthwhile. There's no point in going into schools and continuing with the political rhetoric that has made so many young people not want to vote. Also, the inclusion of celebrities has helped boost the exposure of the brand and the cause so that more people know who they are and what they're about.

Bite The Ballot needs to (and I'm sure it will) continue to spread the word by encouraging and educating in a way that shows how important politics is and how it affects young people's lives. The 'Leaders Live' interviews were a great success and gave young people a platform to see what each party stood for just by watching the interviews on YouTube. Although 'Leaders Live' may not have attracted non-voters, it certainly helped undecided voters in choosing whether to vote or not. The use of making one day a national registration day also seems to have been very effective with vast numbers of young people taking part. Bite The Ballot do not need me telling them what they should do next as I'm pretty sure that they have a clear idea of how to continue their great work. In my opinion though, further celebrity endorsements and the use of Twitter are certainly the most effective ways to go about it.

Television Debates

The first ever live television debate for a British election was during the 2010 general election campaign. The leaders of the three largest parties at the time, Cameron, Brown and Clegg, debated face-to-face about their policies. In total, there were three debates, each one with a different policy theme. The first was broadcasted on 15th April 2010 on ITV and concerned domestic affairs. The second was a week later on Sky and the topic was foreign affairs. The third and final debate was a further week later and was shown on the BBC with the leaders debating economic issues. The first series of televised debates pushed our political campaign further towards the 21st century as well as copying the same aspects of the American campaign trail.

Five years later and the television debates took over the campaign. They became the centrepiece of the entire election. But, they weren't easily devised as David Cameron stated his issue of having Nigel Farage included but not Natalie Bennett. Therefore, the broadcasters decided to include all seven major political parties of England, Wales and Scotland. However, there was a call for a head-to-head between Miliband and Cameron, but Cameron refused for unknown reasons. The televised debates during the 2015 general election campaign were engaging and popular. They provided a fantastic discussion across all platforms with the debates being shown on YouTube as well as television.

The first live debate of the election was broadcasted on both Channel 4 and Sky News. It wasn't so much of a debate though, more of a Q&A session of audience participation with Miliband, Cameron and Paxman. The master of the political interviews, Jeremy Paxman, made Cameron look like an evil dictator by grilling him on food banks and zero-hours contracts whilst Miliband left in a slightly better state. The headline debate was broadcasted by ITV and included all seven leaders of the major political parties. The debate didn't give the electorate any new knowledge about policies or potential coalitions, but it certainly engaged people with the campaign and kept them talking about it days after. The debate that provided the most talking points was the opposition debate on BBC One that included Miliband, Farage, Sturgeon, Bennett and Wood. Here we saw Nicola Sturgeon openly ask Ed Miliband for a Labour/SNP coalition. Miliband strongly declined Sturgeon's offer and made many speculate whether he was firstly telling the truth and secondly, whether he'd win a majority on his own.

As well as debates with a generalised audience, there were Q&A sessions for young people in the form of 'Leaders Live', 'Freespeech' and 'Stand Up And Be Counted'. All gave young people a chance to grill the leaders and representatives of the major parties in the hope that they'd get young people to vote for them. So, these already exist for young people but as I've stated before, the only young people that will attend or watch television debates are those that are already interested in politics. What we need are television debates that young people who aren't interested in politics can take part in or watch. And, the use of social media will be an indispensable part of this. What television debates do is bring in audiences that don't usually know what each party stands for. I believe they also add an extra spark to the usually dull campaign trail. If we want young people to be engaged, television debates are ideal. The more we have, the better. Television and cross-platform interconnectivity is what 'Blair's children' know after all.

Russell Brand

Russell Brand's influence has been deemed negative and unhelpful. Many suggest that Brand is doing nothing to help people engage with politics. The *Independent*, the BBC, IBTimes and the *Huffington Post* all ran articles about a YouGov poll and negative effects celebrities have on politics. Brand was ranked top of the list as the celebrity to have the most damaging influence on politics closely followed by Jeremy Clarkson. Brand divides opinion as his boisterous, loudmouth and personally declared narcissistic persona puts many people off. An article in *Prospect* magazine in October 2014 declared distaste for Brand as they went with the headline "No, Russell Brand, You're No Noam Chomsky." Brand himself would tell you he's nowhere near the intellect of Chomsky and he's not trying to be him. Chomsky has had a major influence on Brand's beliefs, thoughts and writing but he would never suggest that he's anywhere near the height of Chomsky.

Brand's stance on not voting came to air when he was infamously interviewed by Paxman on *Newsnight*. This caused many people to unnecessarily scream and shout that he was having a damaging effect on young people in particular. Days prior to the 2015 general election, Brand interviewed Ed Miliband

and urged people to vote for Labour as they were the least-worst option. His stance changed in the heat of the campaign from frustrated, apathetic non-voter to angry anti-Conservative endorser. Political commentators, the press and even celebrities such as Brian May all discouraged Brand's stance on voting. They all declared that Brand was putting people off politics with his ironically truthful messages.

However, I completely disagree that Russell Brand has put people off politics. What Russell Brand has done is get people talking. People who would have never spoken about politics before, people who have been totally disenfranchised by the established elite and young people who are experiencing this new hobby of political activism. Let's dispel the myth that people agreeing with Brand have been put off from voting. Brand's 'followers' were already disengaged with politics and didn't vote in the first place. They simply have a figure that represents them now. As for young people, they are as divided as the rest of us. In fact, the division isn't black-and-white here. One side doesn't like Brand and thinks his message is 'stupid', the middle don't like politics and weren't going to vote even before Brand's input and the third side have been engaged by Brand and he has brought out a side of political activism that nobody else could.

I would argue that the 'Green surge' that Natalie Bennett continues to talk about (although now it's the Green surge 2) was slightly down to the influence of Brand's left-wing ideological messages. Brand's YouTube channel, *The Trews*, has over a million subscribers with over 100 million total views on his videos and according to the *Daily Mail* he made £230,000 from sales of his book *Revolution* in only 11 days. People are listening to Brand. There's also an ironic point here. The haters of Brand have been forced to declare and explain why they have their political beliefs and how Brand's are 'wrong'. In turn, those who don't want Brand to share his political activism with the public are heating the debate up and making Brand more infamous and popular. Brand has taken away the alienation and academic exclusivism of political discourse for those who were previously apathetic or showed disinterest. You may not agree with his left-wing messages but if you want young people to start engaging with politics, Brand has certainly done that.

But is Brand a solution to get young people voting? The more young people that engage with the subject, the more likely they are to go on and vote in the future. Brand's left-wing messages have influenced young people into voting Green and I would argue some in Scotland for SNP. Ironically, I don't think his direct message to tell people to vote Labour helped at all. I don't believe that his 'Trewsers' agreed with him on this point, and they either voted Green or didn't vote at all. Brand needs to continue to indirectly get people to vote for the left (Green and SNP) and stay away from telling people who to vote for like a younger, English, bearded Rupert Murdoch.

Brand is a solution and the political activism that has come out of his campaign has and will continue to get people engaged and ultimately voting. Forget that he tells people how pointless it is to vote. We seem to believe that young people are incapable of their own thoughts and if Brand says something like "don't vote" or "voting is pointless" that they're instantly going to do it. What I have found is that it's quite the opposite and Brand has, even if he didn't mean to, engaged people with politics.

Online Voting

A recent survey commissioned by *BBC Newsbeat* suggested that 63 per cent of young people would vote if it could be done online or through an app. Many critics of this venture argue that it's open to political fraud. And yet, these people are happy enough to use online banking or even use a mobile banking app on their smart phones or tablets. I would also argue that postal votes are far more susceptible to fraud than online voting and according to the BBC, 15 per cent of the electorate use postal votes. Not only are postal votes handled by at least half a dozen people but they are also far more susceptible to intimidation as many fill them out in the presence of family members. In an article on the *Mirror* online in April 2015, it was argued that "the key issue holding back the introduction of electronic voting is making sure that hackers and other cybercriminals can't wreck the system." The article also states that the Speaker, John Bercow, is an advocate for online voting and he wants it in place by 2020.

We live in an advanced technological age and our electoral system is forty years behind us. It seems illogical to rule out the prospect of online voting as it would almost certainly get more young people voting. Not only would it be simple and easy, it would interest them far more with the use of their smart phone, tablet or computer. Obviously those without access to any of the above or the internet would still be welcome to vote in person or via the post. People fear change and they like traditions. Completely changing the way we vote would cause a riot amongst the older generation as voting is seen as an event where you go down to the polling station and cross a box. But, we have to move forward and forget about traditions. Democracy should go with the times like everything else. You walk into a local branch of your bank these days and it's all been modernised with far fewer people staffing the counters. Supermarkets are constantly adding self-checkouts and abolishing manned ones. Everything is becoming high-tech and we have to push our electoral system into the 21st century by introducing a form of E-voting.

The Digital Democracy Commission (DDC) set up in 2010 by John Bercow has been tasked with looking into modernising the way we in Britain vote. The DDC website states "Some people said that the inconvenience of having to vote in person was off-putting and suggested that online voting would help to increase voter turnout." Two countries already use online voting and this could help us see how it can be implemented. At the 2014 European elections in Estonia, 31.3 per cent voted via the online system and in the United Arab Emirates, online voting is accessible nationwide. Other countries have introduced online voting but not on a nationwide scale. Some like the United States and Australia have implemented online voting for parts of the country.

Compulsory Voting

Forcing people to vote may, ironically, seem like the most undemocratic thing one could do, but it's certainly effective at increasing voter turnout. Compulsory voting works by implementing a fine if the voter doesn't cast their vote. It doesn't necessarily mean you have to vote for somebody as you can opt out of the election beforehand if your political apathy is too great to make a decision. Many people already cast a 'no vote' and would obviously be even more inclined to do so after the introduction of compulsory voting. Voter turnout would naturally increase as many wouldn't want to receive a fine.

Voting is already compulsory in over thirty countries worldwide with it being enforced in thirteen of them. In Argentina, you are obliged to vote if you are between the ages of 18 and 70 years old. Over-70s are immune from the compulsory voting system due to possible health issues and inaccessibility. They are at virtue to opt out of voting but this must be done at least 48 hours before the election and they must do so before every election if they do not wish to participate. Australia are stricter than Argentina where everyone over the age of 18 must vote or face a $20 fine or even jail time. Brazil has compulsory voting for citizens between the ages of 18 and 70 but only if they are 'literate', making it far more ineffective at raising voter turnout due to the vast illiteracy in Brazil. In North Korea, the entire country is legally obliged to vote but they only have the choice of one candidate. All political parties are banned in North Korea but for the Democratic Front for the Reunification of the Fatherland. At the 2014 elections, they received 100 per cent of the vote with a turnout of 99.97 per cent. If North Koreans fail to vote or deliberately cast a 'no vote' by marking the paper outside of the box for the sole party, the voter will face harsh action. Other countries such as Ecuador, Peru, Luxembourg and Cyprus all have enforced compulsory voting. In Turkey, Egypt, Greece, Mexico and Paraguay, it is compulsory to vote but it isn't general enforced by anybody. In Lebanon, it is also compulsory to vote but only Lebanese men have such a right. Compulsory voting is also present in France but only for the senate elections.

If compulsory voting was introduced in Britain, there would be a liberal outcry from the centre as it would be seen as technically infringing human rights. The addition of a 'none of the above' box below every candidate would lessen the ruckus and it would mean apathetic voters or even voters that don't understand politics could have their say and at the same time, increase voter turnout. However, I don't think compulsory voting will ever become something in centre-leaning Britain as there would be too big of an outcry against the illiberalness of it. Also, the implantation of a body that would hunt down non-voters would cost money that could be better suited elsewhere at a time of austerity and welfare cuts.

Electoral Reform

After the 2015 general election, the need for electoral reform was self-evident. For every UKIP MP elected, it took 3.8 million votes, and 1.1 million for every Green candidate. Whereas every Conservative MP took only 34 thousand and every Labour, 40 thousand. UKIP gained twelve per cent of the vote but only won one seat even though their electoral share was more than the SNP and the Liberal Democrats combined and they came away with a total of 64 seats. (56 SNP and 8 Lib Dem.) The reason for this was the first-past-the-post system and we are all very much aware of this.

The established elite will declare how any change could allow 'radicals' to sneak into parliament and will state that a coalition government isn't good for the country. Firstly, if people want to vote for 'radicals', then so be it. Government should represent the views of the people not what established politicians think is best for us. And secondly, the Conservatives and Liberal Democrats will reputedly argue that the former coalition government was very successful and they worked harmoniously in power 'for the good of the country'. The established elite are just scared of losing their safe seats that some have held for over twenty years.

If a promotional system was introduced, we would have a government that truly represented the voice and will of Britain instead of what we currently have; a dismembered, dispropor-tionate and elitist House of Commons. One of the main reasons why people in general don't vote is because they are fully aware that their vote probably won't impact on the outcome in their constituency. Especially in safe seats that the Tories, for example, will always reclaim no matter the overall feeling around the country. But, even in most marginals, people still won't vote because it's either Labour or Conservative. If for instance they wanted the Lib Dems but knew they didn't stand a chance, they will either vote tactically or stay at home.

With the introduction of a proportional system, every vote will matter. Every vote will make an impact. For those that don't vote because they know their favoured party won't succeed, they will certainly have a reason to make the journey to the polling station. It would see a drastic end to the frustrating and hated tactical voting that has cemented our country into the first-past-the-post system and a two-party format. It's overdue and a long time coming but there really is a push for a reform now with the coalition of Green, UKIP and other parties demanding an electoral referendum before 2020. If proportional representation finally becomes a reality for the British electoral system, more young people will certainly vote as they will see the importance of their voice. And, not only will it get more young people voting but more people across every demographic. Britain will be fairly represented by politicians that the majority actually want and chose by the means of a fair voting system.

Abolishment of the Voting Register

In order to vote in the Britain, one needs to be registered. In 2013 the Individual Electoral Register was introduced which took effect in 2014. It meant that the head of the household was no longer required to register every member of the family that was eligible to vote. Instead it was up to the individual to register themselves. Research carried out by the electoral commission showed that over 7.5 million people weren't registered to vote in 2014. Although registering to vote is a generally easy process, many are put off by having to register in order to do something that they either dislike or don't want to do. It just seems like a lot of effort for something that won't even matter because of the defunct voting system. There was a major push towards getting people to register before the 2015 general election with campaigns on the radio and television. On the final day to register before the 2015 election more than 485,000 people registered to vote. And, as mentioned, the push from Bite The Ballot also convinced many to register before the deadline.

If we didn't have to register to vote, it would certainly remove any reason for not voting relating to the electoral register. Although I'm sure the electoral commission would find it extremely difficult to organise an election, there would certainly be a slightly higher turnout. However, abolishing the register wouldn't have a huge impact. I think if you wanted to vote, you would get around to registering. If you're not that set on voting and register anyway, the odds are you still probably won't vote. I've known people who were adamant that they were going to vote but before they knew it, the deadline to register was looming and they simply couldn't be bothered to do so.

Therefore, I do believe that the register does prove to be an obstacle for some as any slight inconvenience such as registering is enough to put some people off the entire process. Some didn't even know that you had to register in order to vote. Before they'd decided who they wanted to vote for, the deadline had passed and they were unable to take part. Also, having a deadline so close to the election day can make the process rushed and disarranged with some people in the last election registering in time but failing to receive their polling cards. Although you don't technically need a polling card in order to vote, first-time voters won't necessarily know this and will think that they can't vote. As we've literally just had reform regarding the electoral register, I don't see further changes coming any time soon. Also, I don't think they'll scrap the voting register in the foreseeable future as some say it's a necessary tool for organising an election. But, I do believe that further change is needed here and scrapping it completely would get rid of any blockades or obstacles that many see as too time-consuming to jump over.

Ability to Hold MPs to Account

The ability to hold politicians to account is important. There isn't currently any structure in place where the electorate can do this. MPs can get away with anything and the only person that can discipline them is the leader of the party. This is usually with the removal of ministerial jobs but if they are simply a backbench MP, they can't be forced to resign by the party leader. Honourable (and I use that term loosely) men will resign if there is a big enough call for their departure. This is something that UKIP MP Douglas Carswell has strongly campaigned for as he, like the rest of us, is fed up of established politicians getting away with anything under the sun. Having a system in place where we can recall MPs if they act unprofessionally, or if they break their manifesto promises, will certainly give people more hope that politicians will do what they originally campaigned for.

Barack Obama & Boris Johnson

When Barack Obama ran for leader of the Democrats and then president of the United States, Americans who had never voted before turned out en masse to support Obama. America was overcome in a furor of excitement and hope. Not since JFK had there been such a buzz for an American politician with the commotion spreading worldwide and turning Obama into an international celebrity. He defeated Hilary Clinton in his bid to become the leader of the Democrats and then subsequently defeated John McCain to become the president. America truly engaged with politics because of the prospect of having not simply the first black president, but a president that understood everyday Americans.

Obama was elected and now he is a global icon. Although his impact for America has actually been minimal with so much focus on 'Obamacare', he has made people vote that would have never voted before. People in the Hispanic and black communities especially see Obama as a man that will stick up for their needs and deliver for their communities. His charisma has also engaged a number of young Americans with politics as they see him as a celebrity more than a politician. Whether that's a good thing or bad thing, the end result is still that Obama has engaged more young people with politics than any other president would be able to do today.

In comparison in the United Kingdom, Boris Johnson can be said to have had the same effect. Johnson is quintessentially British and yet he is Britain's most favoured politician. He comes across as a bumbling idiot with his stupid hair and pot belly, but his charisma is similar to Obama's. Although Johnson hasn't been able to attract the entire country's vote yet, he certainly will when he inevitably becomes the next leader of the Conservative party. When that time comes, he will certainly attract voters that have never turned out before. The difference between him and Obama though is that Obama seems to connect with his electorate. Johnson simply engages them through comedic personality. He's as posh as a coat hook at Eton but emits this aura of divine charisma that the electorate are eager to vote for en masse. I've heard so many people say "If Johnson was the leader of the Conservatives, I'd vote for him." Even people that are concretely left-wing with instilled hatred for the Tories will completely change for the chance to vote for Johnson and see him as prime minister.

Politicians like Obama and Johnson, although pretty different in comparison, do exactly the same thing. They both engage voters and attract them with their extraordinary charisma. There's no doubt that we need more politicians like them who become worldwide celebrities in order to engage the electorate. Moreover, the celebrity image seems to engage young people even more than the other demographics as 'Blair's children' live in the world of celebrity social media with the interconnected platforms of Twitter, Facebook and Instagram. The frustrating thing is, politicians like this are one in a million and it's unfeasible to have more than one Johnson or Obama at one time.

Celebrity Power

Celebrities have more power than ever before. Through the form of social media, everything they say, do and support is filtered into our digital lives and makes an impact upon us whether we believe it to or not. Although many will suggest that social media has produced celebrities who are of limited talent or are only famous due to scandals or sex tapes, their power is far greater than those talented individuals of the 50s and 60s that we like to discuss. The internet has given the opportunity of fame to anyone with the idea of being 'Twitter famous' or a 'YouTuber' actually more prominent in our lives than most pop stars, film stars or sports personality. But 99 per cent of the new generation of celebrities are young people. It's very rare that you get a 50-year-old woman being known on Twitter for doing absolutely nothing.

But celebrities, in the way we knew them in the 90s, have become as prominent on social media as much as anyone else and they attract a similar demographic of young people. The most followed person on Twitter is Katy Perry with over 70 million followers. Justin Bieber trails second with over 64 million followers and third is Barack Obama's office with over 60 million followers. The first European on the top 100 most followed accounts is Portugal's Cristiano Ronaldo with half the number of followers of Katy Perry: 35 million at number 13. The first Brit on the list doesn't appear until number 24 with Harry Styles and his 24 million followers. All of these celebrities can now influence millions of people like never before in less than 140 characters. But it's not simply classic celebrities that have the power to do this; as stated, anyone can if they have enough followers. British YouTuber Alfie Deyes, who goes by the name of 'Pointless Blogs', has almost 2 and a half million followers and his girlfriend Zoe Sugg, who goes by the name of 'Zoella', has over 3 million followers. They are the two most popular YouTubers in Britain and have a collective reach of over 5.5 million people with most of them being under the age of 25.

During the 2015 general election campaign, some YouTubers were invited to take part in the 'Leaders Live' interviews and grill the leaders and representatives of the main political parties. As well as social-media presence, many political parties have celebrity followers. Martin Freeman, Michael Sheen, Jo Brand,

David Tennant and Steve Coogan all support Labour and helped campaign for them during the 2015 general election. Brian May, Alistair McGowan and Joanna Lumley all support the Green Party. Gary Barlow, Simon Cowell and Vinnie Jones have all vocalised their support for the Conservatives. Hugh Grant, Colin Firth and Richard Dawkins all came out in support for Nick Clegg during the 2010 general election. Celebrities have a voice that can be heard by millions of people. They have an influence that can change outcomes of elections. To harness this power, we need celebrities that young people admire and follow so that they become as engaged as them. YouTubers are the ones who hold enough influence in young people's lives to make this happen. They are who young people listen to.

Lower the Voting Age

At 16 in Britain you begin to pay tax, you can join the armed forces and you can get married. But you can't have your say on any of these matters in parliament. There are over 1.5 million 16 and 17 year olds that are denied the right to vote as the voting age in Britain is currently 18 years old. After the 2015 general election, there has been a huge push to lower the voting age to 16 for elections and referenda. The push has come since the voting age was lowered in Scotland for the independence referendum. During that period, Scotland was gripped in a political frenzy with the entire country talking about the referendum. Old and young people alike would discuss the pros and cons of leaving the United Kingdom in everyday conversations as if they were discussing last night's *X Factor* or *EastEnders*. 17 year olds who turned 18 before the general election and had the chance to vote in the independence referendum were now politically active and this made them want to vote again. But 16 year olds who voted in the independence referendum were left feeling reclusive as they weren't old enough to vote in the 2015 general election.

The Green party especially are campaigning for the voting age to be lowered and desperately want 16 and 17 year olds to have their say in the upcoming EU referendum. It doesn't seem fair that some people have already had the chance to vote in an EU referendum in 1975 and will get another chance to decide our future but 16 and 17 year olds have never had their say. The EU referendum is the perfect opportunity to lower the voting age as the Scottish referendum was. The turnout will speak for itself and will most definitely breathe political life into another probable lost generation.

By denying 16 and 17 year olds the vote, we are telling them that they aren't mature enough to have their say. And yet, we allow them to join the armed forces and get married at the same age. It seems ridiculous that 16 and 17 year olds will start paying tax but not have a say about how much tax they should pay at the time of a general election. If the voting age was lowered to 16, young people would start their political careers at a stage in life when they are still open to embracing new concepts. At 18, you're far more assured about what you like. Granted, people do change dramatically by the age of 18 but 16 year olds are far more susceptible to new interests. If we allow young people to start their political interest sooner, they're much more likely to firstly gain an interest and secondly, hold that interest into their later life. The Scottish referendum proved that lowering the voting age introduced voting to a generation that may have been lost due to their lack of interest in politics. I think it's a certainty that the voting age will be lowered soon. The call is too great to ignore and as we move ever closer to the centre of the political spectrum, age equality will have to be dealt with as much as any other social inequalities.

Political Education

In Britain, we currently don't have political education included in our national curriculum in schools. The closest thing we have to this is Citizenship lessons where pupils might get taught about which countries are in the European Union at the very most. Most schools do participate in student elections where class presidents, head pupils or prefects are elected. This is done using a first-past-the-post system and directly copies our electoral system in the sense of how to vote by marking a cross next to a name on a piece of paper and placing it into a ballot box. This is the very limited experience that young people get regarding politics and quite frankly, it's completely ridiculous.

During the 2015 general election, Twitter was awash with 18 to 24 year olds stating their lack of knowledge of politics and how they wished it was taught in schools so that they could participate. It was also awash with the same demographic stating their dislike for the election with tweets suggesting that they don't like politics because they don't understand it. Granted that in most school Citizenship lessons, pupils do debate political matters without the pupils actually knowing what they are being taught. For example, pupils might debate the death penalty or NHS employees' pay. They are taught these things outside of any subject matter that would suggest politics and therefore I think many young people don't realise that they have been taught some politics. If it became a subject on its own, similar to Citizenship with no exam at the end of the year, I think pupils would actually embrace it. Many do want to be taught the basics so that they have a fundamental knowledge about how to vote when they turn 18.

If the voting age is inevitably lowered to 16, it is vitally important that politics is taught in schools as many will still be in school when they can vote. As I have suggested before, organisations such as Bite The Ballot do tremendous work by going into schools and teaching politics. However, this isn't enough. Bite The Ballot can't be at every school five days a week. We need an initiative from each school to copy the Bite The Ballot formula and teach it themselves. Of cause, we can't rely on the government to set up any type of lesson in schools as one gets the feeling that they don't want every pupil to be taught politics. Politics is taught in some private schools and this is where we see elitism begin to take shape. The people at the top receive a leg-up even before they leave school and the rest of us are left fending for ourselves in the world of politics. We need an equal political system and this can be started by making an equal education system and introducing politics lessons into our schools.

I really don't see any objection here and neither do the pupils. The objection ultimately seems to come from the top. Mainly the government's refusal to deal with the question. Having a good education system is fundamental to the success of our country. Making our education system equal and comprehensive is key to the growth of our electorate. We need to push for political education from as young as possible because the sooner we get children interested in politics, the more likely they are to become engaged with the subject and turn out to vote when they are eligible. Many will argue that "I wasn't taught politics at school and I vote." The difference is, the rest of us (excluding myself of course) aren't one of 'Blair's children'. The decline in political interest and turnout needs to be met at a young age because technology is only going to improve, making 'Blair's children' evolve into Cameron's children.

More Diverse Representation

Diversity in our government is something that we really struggle with. We fail to have representative numbers of different races, genders, sexualities and ages in the Commons and it has an impact on the way we see our government. We're not looking for complete 50:50 equality here. We're looking for a fair representative government that mirrors the population of Britain instead of what we currently have with a top-heavy group of white heterosexual older men.

However, getting a more representative government isn't an easy task as politics isn't attractive to every demographic. We currently have and always have had so many white men because they are part of the established elite of Britain. They were born into the establishment and gained political power though knowing people and going to public school and Oxbridge rather than working their way up from a poor, working-class, comprehensive-schooled, real-world background. The people we want to get into our government will have had actual jobs before politics. They would have worked real hours for little reward just so they can support themselves and their families. This is opposed to the established elite of our country that go straight into politics after university or after a job with elitist links such as banking or journalism. (Both of which are equally elitists and have more control of British politics than the government would care to admit.)

The question here isn't whether people want to vote for people other than white older men. The question is why aren't enough ethnic, LGBT or younger people standing as candidates in the first place? There has been an increase in all four categories since the 2010 election with 191 female candidates being elected. However this still isn't good enough. This should be 50/50. The number of female MPs currently stands at 29 per cent. Although more women than ever before stood in the 2015 general election, the increase needs to be seen in elected candidates. Moreover, the number of black, Asian and minority-ethnic MPs was up to 38 from 27 in 2010. But this is simply not good enough.

To combat this, foundations need to be laid at the routes. That starts with the previous solution of a political education but it also needs to happen socially as ethnic minorities aren't supporting the idea of becoming a politician as much as the established elite of this country is. That can also be said for the

LGBT community. The idea of a transgender politician isn't widely accepted, and therefore, the idea of becoming a politician isn't even thought about by the community. Getting younger people to become MPs is slightly harder as politics is something that is commonly down to experience and age. But, that does not mean young people can't be MPs as Mhairi Black showed by becoming the youngest MP since 1667 at the age of 20. A more diverse government would introduce politics to a wider spectrum of younger people. People of the LGBT community, the ethnic community as well as young women would see people just like them standing up in the Commons and fighting to empower their communities and fellow peers.

Abolishment of Prime Minister's Questions

Every Wednesday, the prime minister plays the starring role in the great British pantomime that is Prime Minister's Questions. Like a well-rehearsed play, the prime minister takes centre stage and answers questions from his opposition as well as members of his party. The leader of the opposition goes head to head with the prime minister in a dual of wit and farce. Nothing can truly compare to the extravert performers in blue or black suits fighting their corners with pages of appalling satire and pointless observations. This live spectacle is broadcasted on *BBC Parliament* and rakes in the most viewers out of any other programme on that channel.

But people don't watch it to hear new policy announcements or to see how parliament works as neither of these things happen. People tune into Prime Minister's Questions for the entertainment like any other reality television programme. The spectacle is respectfully hated by the public as they don't believe that elected members of parliament should act like children, shouting at each other as if they were in a classroom with a supply teacher. David Cameron himself says how much he hates

Prime Minister's Questions. He said whilst being interviewed by Sky News' *AskTheLeaders* series: "At five minutes to twelve every Wednesday, I can tell you, I put my head in my hands," he said. "It's a nightmare." This isn't the first time that Cameron has declared his distaste for PMQs but you really wonder if he actually believes what he says. Watching Cameron during PMQs, you get a sense that he is in his element among his peers and friends acting as the headline comedian at the Edinburgh Festival making observations about the opposition's faults and failed policies. Cameron has also said that PMQs is good because it does "enforce some accountability" to the prime minister as he must be clued up on every subject matter and policy. Therefore, I think Cameron does actually want PMQs to stay and his talk of hating it is solely about the adrenaline he gets before he goes on 'stage'.

There are some that suggest that the crazy behaviour of politicians in PMQs is a good thing as a rowdy parliament means the politicians are up for a debate and that ultimately helps improve policy-making. However, there's a difference between strong, electrifying debate and a farce. PMQs is the latter and cannot be seen as a healthy thing for our parliament. It does nothing to improve policies or introduce new laws. The frustrating spectacle of PMQs annoys the public deeply and makes many dislike politics completely. When we see our elected MPs shout at each other with smiles upon their faces, childish noises coming from their mouths and finger-pointing that you'd be told off for doing by your mother, it puts the entirety of politics into a ball of ridiculous buffoonery that you'd expect to see on Cartoon Network in the early noughties.

PMQs isn't going to inspire anyone into voting. In fact it does the complete opposite and puts so many people off from respecting them as politicians and, I guess, as human beings too. We need to abolish PMQs once and for all so that politics isn't seen as this pathetic pantomime and instead we see it as a respectable place where hard work is done to improve our country. Moreover, a 'people's question time' would be far more beneficial so that the electorate can grill the prime minister on current affairs and current policies. This would then allow David Cameron to have something that would keep him up-to-date with his own policies (even though he surely should know them anyway) and the prime minister would also be accountable to us, the public.

Abolishment of Commons Traditions

The House of Commons hasn't changed much in the past 100 years. The traditions have almost stayed the same and the way parliament works also looks pretty similar. Drastic changes are needed in order to make parliament, and politics itself, look up-to-date, modern and ready to embrace the 21st century albeit over 15 years late. When the SNP gained 50 seats at the 2015 general election, many of them didn't have a clue what to expect in the House of Commons. When an SNP MP made a statement in the chamber that went down well with their fellow Scottish nationalists, the speaker had to stop them all from clapping as it has been a 'tradition' in the chamber not to clap. To a normal person, they clap when they agree with someone or something. But in the Commons, a "here, here" is deemed correct and the quintessentially British nature of the chamber is maintained. The pompous and almost arrogant nature of John Bercow was shown quite clearly here towards the Scottish MPs as they either weren't aware of the pathetic tradition or quite rightly didn't agree with it. It's a strange world we live in when shouting is considered more polite than clapping. Moreover, the idea that filibustering is allowed is quite simply ludicrous.

The pageantry of the Commons and the Lords is thought to be a symbol of Britishness and traditional splendour. The Queen's speech typically emphasises both of these beliefs. Both chambers join together and enter the Lords to witness the Queen's speech that opens parliament for the year. The Palace of Westminster becomes a beacon of tradition at this point in the year as the civil servants behind the scenes work tirelessly to get the building ready for the Queen's presence. Moreover, strict traditions are followed scrupulously during the event even though they're utterly pointless and irrelevant to parliament. The simple existence of 'Black Rod' and his duties clearly defines the tedious traditions that the Palace of Westminster continues to maintain. 'Black Rod's' duty during the state opening of parliament is to summon the members of parliament to the House of Lords in order to hear the Queen's speech. However, 'Black Rod' doesn't simply walk into the chamber and ask for them to follow him. Instead he follows a tradition dating back to 1642 and King Charles I where he bangs his ceremonial mace against the door of the Commons, not before they shut it on his face.

They seem to live in a different world all together where traditions are followed and the outside world is forgotten. And, although 'Black Rod's' existence is pointless, the simple gesture of addressing each other as "my right-honourable" shows the world that parliament isn't a place of modern thinking or 21st-century behaviour. This is language that hasn't been used for over one hundred years but it's no surprise that in that period, parliament hasn't change much either. David Cameron was once asked about the archaic language of parliament and he suggested that calling each other by their actual names wouldn't be very professional. Radical changes are needed within the Palace of Westminster full stop. Even the existence of the House of Lords is questionable to democracy. Introducing a radical overhaul of changes into British parliament would stop putting so many people off politics as they wouldn't feel alienated by the system or the traditions. If they spoke like us, acted like us and ultimately thought like us, people would be less likely to be turned off by politics and even more likely to hold a connection to the Palace of Westminster. It would no longer look like a building of old men that speak and act like Charles Dickens, and instead, it would entice people into wanting to vote and wanting to be a part of politics.

Capitalism

I've written a lot about capitalism in this book as well as on my personal blog. My stance is clear and hopefully well known by my readers. Many may not agree with what I say but that's fine. My own personal opinion is that and that alone. It's not a mantra that I'm trying to dogmatically get everyone to believe the same as me. I and many others, though, do believe that capitalism is fatally flawed and needs change. Capitalism only benefits the richest and the elite in society. The people at the bottom, the poor, the disabled, the young, they feel the adverse effects of capitalism the worst. What capitalism does do is gives people an imitation of a dream to strive for at a young age only for it to be silently faded out as we work nine till five for fifty years in order to be comfortable in our old age. Whereas the elite and establishment work when they want until whatever age they please with minimal effort and the life of luxury.

The current generation of young people have been hit hard by capitalism and never before has an entire generation been put on the back-foot at the beginning of their lives due to student loans, soaring rent prices and a housing market that only increases the bank balance of the wealthy and homeowners. UKIP would instantly blame this crashed market on the increase in immigration since 2004 and the open-door policy with former communist countries in Eastern Europe. But UKIP fail to recognise, time and time again, that capitalism is the root cause of young peoples' struggles and not immigration. We live in a country where young people are just as worse off living at home as they would be moving out. The point of living at home is to save up enough money in order to move out. But most young people now aren't in a position to save a penny. This shouldn't be the case and our government should try and fix this. However, the needs of capitalism mean it's not in the government's interest to help young people due to them having the smallest income of every demographic. Nor will they fix it due to the fact that they know young people don't vote. Whereas old people are looked after incredibly to try and win their votes as they know that they most likely will go to the polling station.

Capitalism has failed and it has hurt the youth the hardest. Something must change and tackling the banks is where we must start. The banks help tax evasion. There's no question here. If we can claw back the billions of pounds not paid in tax by transnational corporations and billionaires, we can help out the youth so that they can have a debt-free and secure future. If all of the main political parties showed real intent about tackling tax avoidance, the young might start listening and vote for one of those parties. If politics was seen to work for young people, they wouldn't be so disengaged with the entire pantomime and would see that there are politicians that do want to help them and not only fuel capitalism for personal gain.

Many will suggest that capitalism is here to stay and there is no alternative. They'll also suggest that there isn't a better system. However, the people that suggest this don't want you to believe that a new system can be devised. They want you to think that we have climaxed, peaked, that we can't develop our economic system any further. I'm not necessarily arguing that we need communism. Nor am I arguing that socialism would be better for Britain. What I am suggesting is that we need to make changes to capitalism so that it works for everyone. Changes in regulation. Changes in statute. Changes that will mean young people can have hope and prosperity as they get older. If changes are made, young people might take a look a politics and help change the future of the country.

Rebel Rebel

Chris O'Leary

David Bowie: every single song. Everything you want to know, everything you didn't know.

Paperback: 978-1-78099-244-0 ebook: 978-1-78099-713-1

Cartographies of the Absolute

Alberto Toscano, Jeff Kinkle

An aesthetics of the economy for the twenty-first century.

Paperback: 978-1-78099-275-4 ebook: 978-1-78279-973-3

Malign Velocities

Accelerationism and Capitalism

Benjamin Noys

Long listed for the Bread and Roses Prize 2015, Malign Velocities argues against the need for speed, tracking acceleration as the symptom of the on-going crises of capitalism.

Paperback: 978-1-78279-300-7 ebook: 978-1-78279-299-4

Meat Market

Female flesh under Capitalism

Laurie Penny

A feminist dissection of women's bodies as the fleshy fulcrum of capitalist cannibalism, whereby women are both consumers and consumed.

Paperback: 978-1-84694-521-2 ebook: 978-1-84694-782-7

Poor but Sexy

Culture Clashes in Europe East and West

Agata Pyzik

How the East stayed East and the West stayed West.

Paperback: 978-1-78099-394-2 ebook: 978-1-78099-395-9

Romeo and Juliet in Palestine
Teaching Under Occupation
Tom Sperlinger
Life in the West Bank, the nature of pedagogy and the role of a
university under occupation.
Paperback: 978-1-78279-637-4 ebook: 978-1-78279-636-7

Sweetening the Pill
or How we Got Hooked on Hormonal Birth Control
Holly Grigg-Spall
Has contraception liberated or oppressed women? *Sweetening
the Pill* breaks the silence on the dark side of hormonal
contraception.
Paperback: 978-1-78099-607-3 ebook: 978-1-78099-608-0

Why Are We The Good Guys?
Reclaiming your Mind from the Delusions of Propaganda
David Cromwell
A provocative challenge to the standard ideology that Western
power is a benevolent force in the world.
Paperback: 978-1-78099-365-2 ebook: 978-1-78099-366-9

Readers of ebooks can buy or view any of these bestsellers by
clicking on the live link in the title. Most titles are published in
paperback and as an ebook. Paperbacks are available in traditional
bookshops. Both print and ebook formats are available online.

Find more titles and sign up to our readers' newsletter at
http://www.johnhuntpublishing.com/culture-and-politics.
Follow us on Facebook at https://www.facebook.com/ZeroBooks
and Twitter at https://twitter.com/Zer0Books.